Sports Illustrated

FOOTBALL:

OFFENSE

THE SPORTS ILLUSTRATED LIBRARY

BOOKS ON TEAM SPORTS

Baseball
Basketball
Football: Defense
Football: Offense
Pitching
Soccer

BOOKS ON INDIVIDUAL SPORTS

Bowling
Cross-Country Skiing
Golf
Racquetball
Skiing
Tennis
Track: The Running Events

Tumbling
Women's Gymnastics I:
    The Floor Exercise Event
Women's Gymnastics II:
    The Vaulting, Balance Beam
    and Uneven Parallel Bars Events

BOOKS ON WATER SPORTS

Boardsailing
Canoeing
Scuba Diving

SPECIAL BOOKS

Backpacking
Strength Training

Sports Illustrated
FOOTBALL:
OFFENSE
REVISED EDITION

by BUD WILKINSON

Illustrations by Robert Handville

PERENNIAL LIBRARY

Harper & Row, Publishers, New York
Cambridge, Philadelphia, San Francisco, London
Mexico City, São Paulo, Singapore, Sydney

Photo credits:

For *Sports Illustrated*—Andy Hayt: p. 3; John Iacono: pp. 14, 56, 94, 98, 128; Manny Millan: pp. 16, 21; Manny Rubio: p. 18; Richard Mackson: pp. 30, 54, 92; Peter Read Miller: p. 78; Rich Clarkson: p. 91; Heinz Kluetmeier: pp. 110, 112, 166, 174, 184, 186, 193, 194; Grant Haller: p. 134; Tony Tomsic: p. 176; Jerry Wachter: p. 196; Walter Iooss, Jr.: 204; Bill Jaspersohn: p. 22.

All illustrations by Robert Handville.

All diagrams by Frank Ronan.

Library of Congress Cataloging-in-Publication Data

Wilkinson, Bud, 1916–
   Sports illustrated football, offense

   1. Football—Offense. 2. Football—Coaching.
I. Handville, Robert. II. Sports illustrated
(Time, inc.) III. Title.
GV951.8.W5 1986   796.332′2   84-48204
ISBN 0-06-055008-2   86 87 88 89 90 MVP 10 9 8 7 6 5 4 3 2 1
ISBN 0-06-091267-7 (pbk.)   86 87 88 89 90 MVP 10 9 8 7 6 5 4 3 2 1

Contents

Sports Illustrated
FOOTBALL:
OFFENSE

Keys to Diagrams

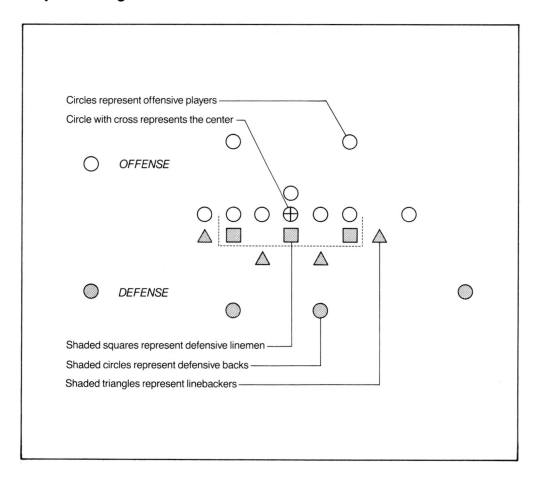

Circles represent offensive players

Circle with cross represents the center

OFFENSE

DEFENSE

Shaded squares represent defensive linemen

Shaded circles represent defensive backs

Shaded triangles represent linebackers

Introduction

Football is a complex game, but its basic elements are simple. That may account for its great and growing popularity at every level of play: little league, junior high school, high school, collegiate, and professional.

Football combines the fundamentals of other familiar sports: the speed of track, the throwing and catching of baseball and basketball, the strength, leverage, and body contact of wrestling and boxing, the kicking of soccer. When these skills are combined in one game in which the tactics and strategies are as complex as those of chess or bridge, the game becomes challenging for players and entertaining for spectators.

The game is divided into three phases—defensive football, the kicking game, and offensive football. This book covers the offensive phase—as well as aspects of the kicking game—and describes the basic individual techniques of blocking and ballhandling. These fundamentals are the same regardless of the offensive formation being used. A player who can effectively execute the fundamentals of his position can use these techniques in any of the popular offensive formations currently in use—the Pro-Set, the I formation, the Veer, the Wishbone.

11

The popularity of various formations changes with the years. Teams that succeed on offense are soon copied by opponents and other admirers.

Yet the statement that there is nothing really new in offensive football remains accurate. Formation changes, with rare exceptions, are simply mutations of ideas used many years ago. For example, at the University of Oklahoma I coached the Split-T formation. The plays we used were diagrammed in a text Amos Alonzo Stagg had written in 1908, before I—not to mention my players—was born. The mutation we used at Oklahoma was to "split" our linemen in order to spread out the defensive players.

In recent years, there have been two major developments in offensive football:

- The increased use of the forward pass.
- The capacity of the offensive team to adjust the "point of attack" *after* the ball has been snapped.

My coach at the University of Minnesota was Bernie Bierman. We did have a number of passes in our offensive plans, but generally we were expected to out-muscle our opposition with our running attack. A thought attributed to the late Jock Sutherland, the great coach of the University of Pittsburgh in the 1930s, clearly illustrates the philosophy prevalent at the time. Supposedly, Jock said, "The forward pass is a cowardly, immoral play." Today, a team that cannot throw the ball effectively has little chance of winning.

With the advent of two-platoon football (until the late 1950s, even professionals had to play both offense and defense), the play of the defensive team became much more sophisticated. In today's game, the offensive team calls a play—and the defensive team does, too! The defense gambles that the play it calls will be effective against the offensive play called. If the defensive call is correct, no yardage can be gained unless the offensive team is able to adjust the point of attack *after* the ball has been snapped.

This is true of both the running game and the passing game, and it has resulted in the increased development and use of "option" offensive football.

For all those wrinkles, football in its purest form remains a physical fight: player against player. As in any fight, if you don't want to fight, it's impossible to win. Thus, morale and attitude remain fundamental ingredients for success.

In offensive football, there are inherent contradictions between players' individual ambitions and their ability to contribute to the team. It is axiomatic that:

- Linemen prefer to play defense because they get more recognition by making tackles than by blocking on offense.

- Backs prefer to play offense because they get more recognition by being ballcarriers than by being defensive players.

Nevertheless, if a team is to reach its potential, each player must be willing to subordinate his personal goals to the good of the team.

Morale and attitude are the bases of success. Given those ingredients, each player will strive to develop the individual techniques and skills needed to play his position. Those skills can then be coordinated to create the most effective offensive team possible within the combined individual potentials of the players.

This text is intended for the developing player, not the highly sophisticated, experienced participant. It does not attempt to examine in-depth the arguments for and against various offensive systems and styles of play. But while football is a complex game of infinite variety, fundamentals remain just that, and the proper execution of these basics, when combined with high motivation and morale, can ensure the success of the individual player and his team.

1

The Balance Between Offense and Defense

All team games have a delicate balance between offense and defense. That balance keeps either offense or defense from dominating the contest.

For example, in baseball the distance of 90 feet from home plate to first base and the distance of 60 feet, six inches from pitcher's rubber to home plate provide the basic balance that keeps the game competitive. If the pitcher's mound were moved 10 feet further back from home plate, the batter would have a great advantage because of the extra time it would take the ball to reach the plate. If first base were moved to 100 feet from the plate, it would be more difficult for the batter to get a hit and even outfielders might be able to throw out the runner at first base.

In football, the balance of the game rests on the advantage the rules give to the defensive player as opposed to the offensive player. Defensive players are allowed almost unlimited use of their hands and arms. This gives them improved body balance, and they can use their hand and arm strength to avoid blockers.

The offensive linemen offset this defensive advantage by knowing *when* the ball will be snapped, giving them a chance to get the jump on their opponent. They also know *where* the play will go,

15

In the balance between offense and defense, the offense knows when the ball will be snapped and where the play will go.

New rules now give offensive players less-restricted use of their hands. One result: improved passing attacks.

telling them which opponent they must block or what pattern they must run.

A few years ago, the rules for blocking by offensive linemen were changed. The old rules required that the linemen keep their hands close to their chest. The new rule allows them to use their hands within the framework of their opponent's body. This has given offensive linemen far greater ability to block their opponents, particularly when they are protecting the passer. The rule change has resulted in improved passing attacks. Before this rule change, games tended to be low scoring because of the stodgier balance between offense and defense. Rarely did a team score more than three touchdowns. Today it is not unusual to have both teams score more than three touchdowns.

In professional football, an additional rule change has been made that further opens up the offensive passing game. Defensive players are allowed to "check" offensive receivers within 4½ yards of the line of scrimmage. After the receiver moves downfield beyond 4½ yards, defensive players cannot make physical contact. This makes it possible for receivers to run unobstructed patterns once they are beyond that imaginary boundary and makes it much easier for them to get open.

This rule change, combined with the more effective pass-protection blocking with offensive linemen using their hands, has made it much easier to throw the ball successfully. In today's game, it is comparatively rare for the combined score of both teams to be less than 40 points.

As a coach, I am not totally in favor of these rule changes, since they have altered the balance that did exist between offense and defense, but the increased scoring seems to be very popular with players, the media and spectators.

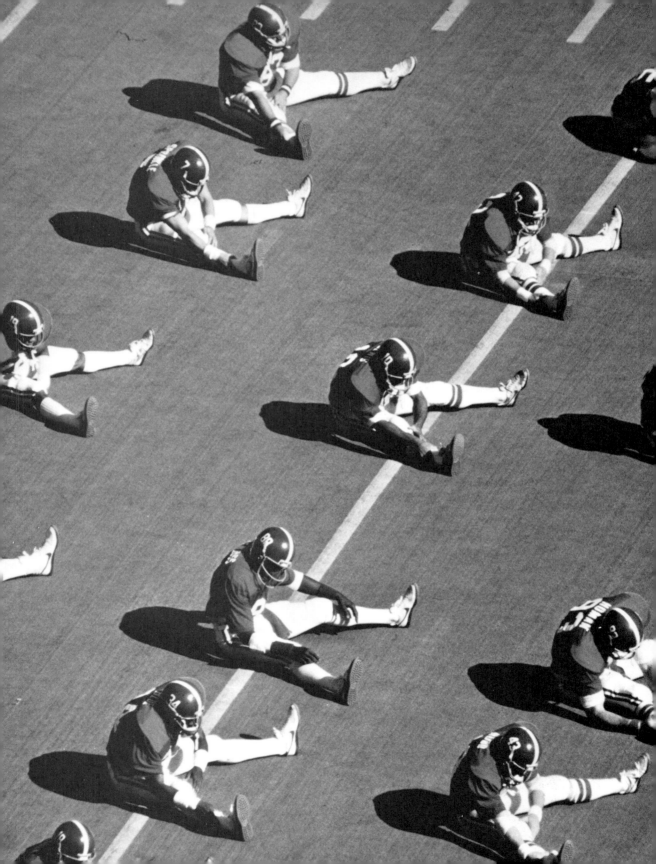

2

Warmup and Conditioning

The most common misconception concerning football is that it is essentially a game of size and strength. It is also a game of speed and reaction. The physical demands of the various offensive positions enable young men of a wide variety of physiques to play successfully. Slightly built young men who have speed of foot and the ability to catch the ball can play well as wide receivers. Heavily built, slower types can be effective interior offensive linemen. Players with athletic ability are needed for the other positions.

A few generalizations about what type of offense a coach should use:

- If the players tend to be big and fast, it doesn't make much difference what formation is used.
- If the players tend to be big and slow, an assaulting type of offense, concentrating on straight-ahead, hard-hitting plays, should be used.
- If the players tend to be small and fast, the coach should use a wide-open attack.

With young players, care should be exercised to avoid physical mismatches. Boys bigger and stronger than others their age should be assigned

19

Stretching before a game or practice helps reduce the risk of muscle pulls.

to the interior line positions. If they are too superior physically, they should be moved up to a stronger arena of competition.

Football is a physical game and the team that hits hardest wins. But leg strength and agility are more important than arm and shoulder strength. And since the team is only as good as its ability to move, young players should work on developing their legs. This can be accomplished by running and by special exercises that should be done after the players have limbered up by stretching.

RUNNING EXERCISES

1. Jog. This loosens the muscles. Players should jog until they break a slight sweat. On cold days, it will be necessary to jog a great deal further to have perspiration begin, which ensures that the muscles have been loosened.

2. Sprint various distances. Begin with five-yard bursts starting from a football stance, and do six to eight sprints. Then, again from a football stance, sprint 10 yards while concentrating on running form. Attempt to lift the knees high and lengthen the stride. Again, six to eight 10-yard sprints should be done. Finally, four 20-yard sprints should be done. On these runs, the player will have time to work carefully on improving his running form by lifting his knees high and using the swing of his arms to balance his body as he attempts to lengthen his stride.

3. Run sideways. To run to the left, keep the shoulders parallel to the direction of movement, cross the right leg over the left, then swing the left leg wide to the left and repeat for a distance of 20 yards. Run back in the opposite direction, crossing the left leg over the right. Again, run about 20 yards: In all, a player should move the 20 yards in each direction three or four times.

4. Run backward. Reach back for the longest possible stride and raise the knees as high as possible while running backward for 20 yards. A player should run the 20 yards backwards three or four times.

SPECIAL EXERCISES

1. From a standing position, raise one leg, grasp the shin, and slowly, without jerking, pull the knee and leg against the chest as high as possible.

Repeat the exercise with the other leg. The player should repeat the exercise with each leg six to eight times.

2. The player does the same exercise lying on his back. Again, six to eight repetitions with each leg.

3. The player lies on his back, his arms extended at shoulder height on either side, and rolls the right leg over and attempts to touch the left palm with the right toes. He then rolls to the left side and touches the right palm with the left toes. Players should do this exercise smoothly without bobbing or straining and move in each direction six to eight times.

4. In a standing position, the player crosses his feet and, while keeping his knees straight, bends from the waist and touches his fingertips or palms to the ground. No bobbing! A player should stretch as far as he can without over-stretching, then cross his legs the opposite way and repeat the exercise.

If the player cannot touch the ground, he should stretch for four to six seconds without bobbing, and then repeat the exercise four to six times. The player's muscles will gradually lengthen from doing this exercise. Within a

Proper conditioning for football should include a well-supervised strength program.

relatively short period of time, the player will be able to touch the ground. Again, I emphasize: the player should not bob as he does the stretch. Over-stretching by bobbing can lead to pulled muscles.

Players should always use the warmup drills listed above, or other calisthenics the coach includes in his own warmup program, before practice begins.

Nautilus and other types of weight machines, as well as free weights (barbells and dumbbells), are available in almost every community. By using these machines and free weights, young athletes can develop all their muscles. The use of the machines and weights, with supervision, can assure the proper muscular development for each player. Note, however, that, owing to growth factors and the possibility of muscle injury, young athletes should not lift weights or use weight machines until they are at least 14 years old.

A player's basic equipment for football.
Shoulder pads, hip pads, and football cleats (left) along with a helmet, face mask, jersey, and padded pants (right) comprise the basic playing equipment for tackle football. All equipment, particularly the helmet, should be of proper fit, and broken or worn-out equipment should not be used.

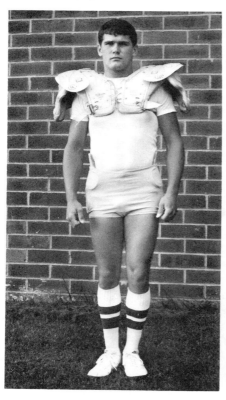 

PROTECTIVE EQUIPMENT

Adequate equipment is a must for participation in tackle football, and the first requirement is that it fit properly. If it hangs loose, it can be dangerous.

Minimum equipment includes a helmet, shoulder pads, and football pants, which include hip pads, thigh pads, and knee pads. Shoes should fit well, but football shoes are not a necessity. Tennis or basketball shoes, while not providing the best traction, are adequate for younger players.

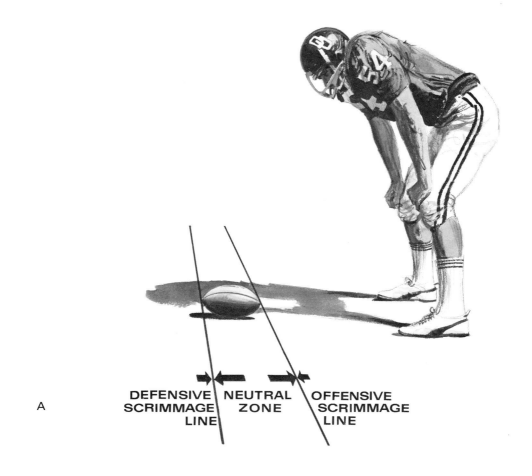

DEFENSIVE
SCRIMMAGE
LINE

NEUTRAL
ZONE

OFFENSIVE
SCRIMMAGE
LINE

A

B

Components of the Offensive Team

Before each play begins, the offensive and defensive teams are separated by the neutral zone, which is the length of the football.

The rules require that at least seven offensive players be on the line of scrimmage. If the coach desires, eight, nine, or even ten men may legally be on the line of scrimmage.

A wide variety of offensive formations are used in modern football. Regardless of the formation, the components of the team are always the same. These are:

1. *"Down linemen,"* including the center, who has the additional duty of snapping the ball. Physically, these men must be strong through their entire bodies. They must possess the strength, balance, and agility to control the line of scrimmage against the defensive team.

2. *Tight ends.* These men are on the line of scrimmage within a yard and a half of a down lineman. Ideally, they should possess the same strength as down linemen. In addition, they should have enough speed to be capable pass receivers. This is a rare combination of physical skills.

3. *Wide receivers.* These men may be on or

25

On the line of scrimmage, the neutral zone is the length of the football (A). No offensive players, except the center, may be ahead of their end of the ball. Defensive players may not be ahead of their end of the ball (B).

behind the line of scrimmage and are at least five yards outside the tight end or down lineman. Ideally, they should possess sprinter's speed. They also must have great balance and faking ability as they run pass patterns so that they can get open against man-for-man pass defenses.

4. *Running backs.* These men are at least four yards behind the line of scrimmage, in position to be handed the ball by the quarterback or catch it if it is tossed to them. They should be fast and elusive and also be effective blockers when they do not carry the ball. Running backs who do not block well cannot make their needed contribution to the team since their blocking ability will play an important role in every running play. Also, it is essential that they be effective pass-protection blockers if the thrower is to have time to deliver the ball.

5. *The quarterback* (or tailback in a Single-wing or Shotgun set). This man is in position to be handed the ball by the center, or in the Shotgun set, catch the ball when the center throws it to him. He is the key to the effectiveness of the offense regardless of which formation is being used. His most needed skills are a strong arm coupled with great peripheral vision so that he can see the entire width of the field on pass plays. Also, if the team is running an "option" attack like the veer or wishbone (which are described in detail later), he must be a strong, elusive, effective ballcarrier.

Every player on the offensive team must master the two most important basic offensive skills. These are the hitting position and proper use of the eyes.

Components of the Offensive Team

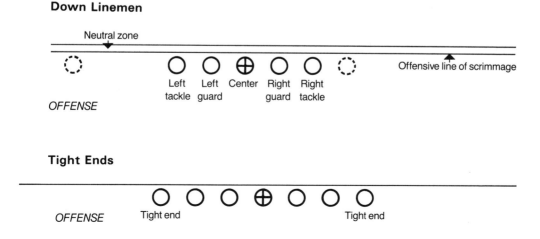

Down Linemen

Neutral zone

Offensive line of scrimmage

Left tackle   Left guard   Center   Right guard   Right tackle

OFFENSE

Tight Ends

OFFENSE   Tight end   Tight end

Wide Receivers

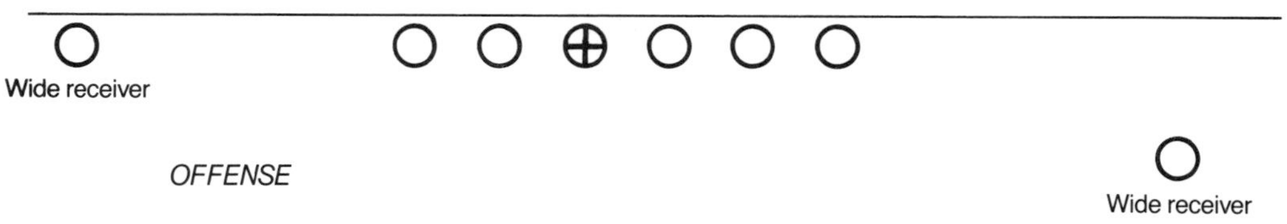

○   ○ ○ ⊕ ○ ○ ○

Wide receiver

OFFENSE

○

Wide receiver

Running Backs

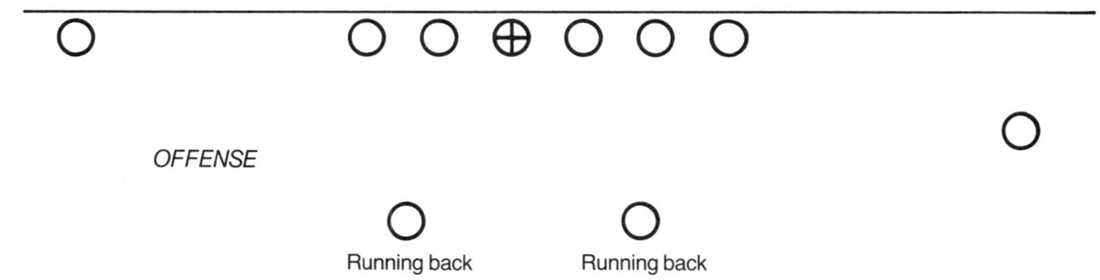

○   ○ ○ ⊕ ○ ○ ○

OFFENSE

○

○   ○

Running back   Running back

The Quarterback

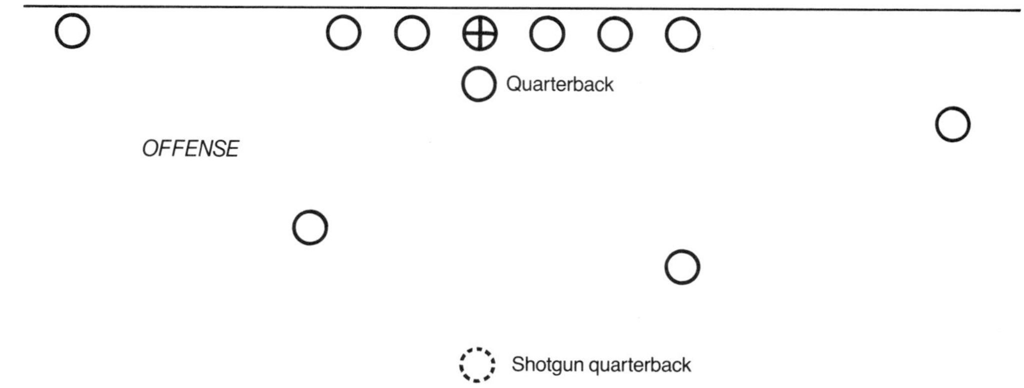

○   ○ ○ ⊕ ○ ○ ○

○ Quarterback

OFFENSE

○

○   ○

⊙ Shotgun quarterback

THE HITTING POSITION

All offensive and defensive contact in football is delivered from the same hitting position. Every football player must understand and practice the proper hitting position until he can move into it accurately just before the moment of contact.

The correct hitting position has the player's feet spread about the width of his shoulders. One foot should be 10 to 12 inches ahead of the other. The knees are bent. The hips are low and the body does not bend from the waist. With the feet in the correct hitting position, the knees bent, and the trunk held straight, the player is in position to use his leg, back, and arm muscles to deliver the blow against his opponent.

The player should always attempt to have his center of gravity lower than that of the opponent he is attacking so that he can raise, lift, and drive the opponent backward as he overpowers him.

The hitting position
Bend your knees about 75 degrees; spread your feet apart about the width of your shoulders. Keep your back straight, your neck bulled. From this coiled position you can use the muscles of your legs, back, abdomen, and shoulders to strike a hard blow, whether playing offense or defense.

USE OF EYES

Good vision is needed to play football well, but it is useless if the player closes his eyes just before contact. If he does, he is blind at the moment his opponent is trying hardest to evade him. With his eyes closed, the player cannot see the evasive moves of his opponent just before contact and may well miss his target.

A quick blink at the moment of contact is inevitable, but constant coaching and practice can teach the player to avoid squeezing and keeping his eyes closed. He can and must learn to see his opponent and adjust to the opponent's movement through the period of contact.

Offensive Line Play

It is a truism that the team that controls the line of scrimmage wins the game. As noted earlier, technically, before the snap of the ball, there are two lines of scrimmage separated by a neutral zone the length of the football. Both teams can move when the ball is snapped. The offense can achieve control of the line of scrimmage by taking advantage of its knowledge of the starting count. This is made possible by flawless stances by all players and a coordinated, explosive start by the offensive linemen.

The offensive linemen are the center, two guards, and two tackles. All of these men must learn to execute the fundamental skills demanded by their positions. The center's skills are the same as the guards' and the tackles' except that he must snap the ball before executing the fundamentals.

The center is always the most important man in the offensive line. He must be big and strong enough to control a defensive man playing directly in front of him as he snaps the ball. If he lacks the physical skills to block this man, the offense will have no chance of being consistently successful. Dave Rimington, the great Nebraska center who is now a fine professional, is an outstanding example of a skillful offensive center.

31

One of a lineman's chief responsibilities is to be the
lead blocker on running plays.

The Stance

The Four-Point Stance

Squat, place both hands on the ground directly under the shoulders, and drop one foot back so that the toe is parallel with the heel or instep of the other foot. Raise your hips until your back is parallel to the ground. Distribute your weight equally on your hands and feet, with enough weight forward to let you charge without having to make any preliminary movement or adjustment.

The offensive guards and tackles usually can play either position and execute the fundamentals described below. In most football offenses, the guards pull to "trap" (entice a defensive player to cross the line of scrimmage in an attempt to penetrate into the backfield—and then hit him from the side to open the hole) or lead a play far more often than do the tackles. Consequently, the guards need greater running ability than do the tackles. This is the only distinction between the two positions, and as stated above, the guards and the tackles must be able to execute all of the fundamentals for offensive line play.

THE STANCE

The four-point stance is used by a few offensive teams that do not require their linemen to pull out—that is, leave their positions after the ball is snapped to run a trap or lead on wide plays. Arkansas and Oklahoma use this stance since the wishbone attack requires the linemen to charge straight ahead on almost all plays.

On certain plays, however, most offensive teams require that their linemen

The Three-Point Stance
Squat and place your right hand on the ground directly ahead of your right knee, dropping your right foot back slightly. (Left-handed players use the left hand and foot.) Raise your hips to make your back parallel to the ground. Distribute your weight equally on the tripod formed by your feet and your hand.

pull to trap or pull to "lead wide" in addition to charging straight ahead to block. These linemen should use the three-point stance, and all linemen should learn it.

STEPPING

From either the four-point or the three-point stance, all linemen must learn to step with either foot. This is a vitally important fundamental. Defensive linemen often play in the gap between two offensive linemen. When a defensive lineman is in the gap to the left of an offensive lineman and the play is designed to go outside the offensive lineman, unless he has the ability to step with his left foot, the defensive lineman will be able to shoot the gap and get "penetration." If the offensive lineman in this situation steps with his right foot, the defensive player will have penetrated before the offensive man's left foot can move.

As a rule, offensive linemen should always step first with the foot closest to the opponent to be blocked. If this man is to the left, step with the left foot. If he is to the right, step with the right foot.

In making a straight-ahead charge, the lineman must move his entire body

Stepping

A

B

The rule of thumb is: Always step first with the foot closest to the opponent to be blocked.

The opponent is to the left. The offensive lineman steps first with his left foot.

C

The opponent is to the right. The offensive lineman steps first with his right foot.

A

B

The Trap Play

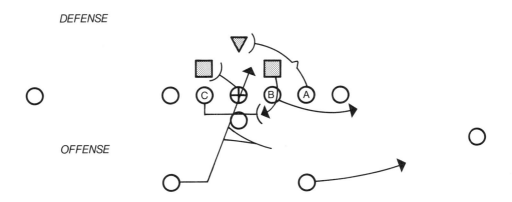

DEFENSE

OFFENSE

Player A fakes a block on the defensive lineman inside of him and then moves downfield to block the linebacker.

Player B pulls to the outside.

Player C executes the trap block.

forward with the snap of the ball. If the buttocks are raised too high, or if there is other body movement before the charge, it will tip off the timing of the start of the play and the blocker will lose the jump on his opponent.

"Trap plays" are designed to take advantage of overly aggressive defensive linemen. Usually, defensive linemen strive to get immediate, fast penetration across the line of scrimmage and into the offensive backfield, to spoil the play being run. The lineman just outside the defensive man to be trapped fakes a block on the opponent and then moves downfield to block the linebacker. The lineman in front of the man to be trapped pulls to the outside. The combination of these two moves entices the defensive linemen to believe a wide play is about to be run, particularly if the quarterback fakes a toss to one of the running backs. The man to be trapped penetrates across the line of scrimmage and becomes an easy target for the offensive lineman who is making the trap block.

In pulling to trap, the offensive lineman takes the three-point stance. To

Pulling to Trap to the Left

LINE OF SCRIMMAGE

trap to the left, he should push back with the hand as the ball is snapped and swing the left foot back about 18 inches while turning his shoulders 45 degrees to the left. Then he should step with the right foot toward the line of scrimmage to maintain an inside angle on the defender to be trapped. To trap to the right, the player should take his first step with the right foot.

When pulling to lead a play wide, the offensive lineman again assumes a three-point stance. To lead to the left, he should push with his hand as the ball is snapped and swing his left foot back about 10 inches and out about 12 inches. Then he should swing the right foot back and away from the line of scrimmage, past the left foot, and circle around to position himself for the block. When pulling to lead to the right, he should move the right foot first.

A player executing the lead block is never positive exactly which man he will block. He moves out as described and blocks the first man who comes to him as he leads around to his outside.

The Lead Block

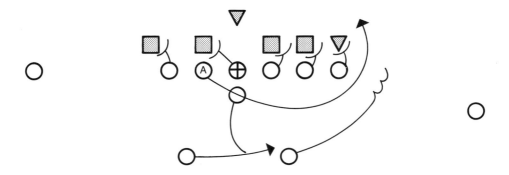

Here, Player A leads a running play wide right.

There are five basic blocks: the one-on-one shoulder block, the double-team block, the "reach" or "scramble" block, the pass-protection block and the open-field block—all designed to control the defense so that the team can advance the ball. The secret to good blocking is to make and maintain contact with the opponent and to have a definite target: the opponent's belt buckle.

The One-on-One Shoulder Block

To execute this block to the left, gauge your distance from the defensive player so that your left shoulder hits on his belt buckle as your left foot hits the ground. Then step past him with your right foot. Follow through by taking shorter steps with your left foot than your right, thereby turning your opponent further and further to the left. When executing a shoulder block to the right, make contact with your right shoulder to his belt buckle as your right foot hits the ground.

The position of the head is of *paramount* importance. Most poor blockers fail to "bull" their neck. Instead of holding their head directly over their shoulders, they tend to tilt it to the outside and look at the ground. If they do this, they lose sight of the opponent and consequently miss the block. *Keep your head up, your neck bulled and your eyes on the target.*

The One-on-One Shoulder Block

The Double-Team Block

This block is used against a defender who is very talented and must be removed as a factor in the play. It is executed by two blockers, the "post" man and the "drive" man, working together.

Let's consider a double-team block to the left. First, the post man steps directly at the opponent with his right foot, aiming his right shoulder at the belt buckle and hitting with just enough force to neutralize the defensive player's charge and gain a standoff with him. At the same time, the drive man steps directly at the opponent with his *left* foot, his target being the belt just inside the defensive player's left hip. He drives at this target with his left shoulder, bringing it into contact with his teammate's right shoulder. Then he steps with his right foot at a 45-degree angle past the hip of the defensive player. Both men then follow through with short, chopping steps—the post man pivoting on his left foot, the drive man taking shorter steps with his left foot than with his right to turn the opponent. The offensive players must keep their shoulders and hips together so that the defensive player cannot pass between them.

The Double-Team Block

The Reach or Scramble Block

This is used to tie up an opponent who is playing outside the blocker so that the play can be run around the defender. To scramble-block to the left, step slightly back and out as far as possible with your left foot. Then step laterally with your right foot and drive your right arm out past the defensive player. As your right arm passes him, put both hands on the ground and crawl on your hands and feet to turn the opponent back inside to the right.

The key to a good scramble block is to get your inside arm beyond the defensive player. This gives you leverage, making it possible to turn him inside. In making this movement, you should punch out your inside arm in an upper-cut manner rather than in a sweeping hook. The uppercut ensures that the arm passes the opponent, whereas the hook motion does not.

The Reach or Scramble Block

The Pass-Protection Block

This block is used to keep the backfield clear so that the quarterback can throw the ball. Move from your stance to the hitting position and let the opponent come to you. As the defender nears the contact area, uncoil and deliver a blow with the heels of your hands just under his shoulder pads. Follow through with your charge, using enough power to knock your opponent back. Then reset yourself in the hitting position and continue to block like this until the pass is thrown.

A   B

The Pass-Protection Block
To block legally, the offensive lineman (dark jersey) keeps his hands within the area of the defender's body.

An Illegal Pass-Protection Block
The offensive lineman's hand is outside the area of the defender's body.

The Open-Field Block

This block is made against an opponent who has time and room to move to either side before you reach him. Again the key is to *make and maintain contact with the defensive player.* Usually there is enough room for the ballcarrier to get past the opponent to either side, so take your man the "easy" way: If the opponent is protecting to the left, take him left, and vice versa. The technique is either that of the shoulder block or that of the scramble block.

A   B

The Open-Field Block
The key to effective open-field blocking is to make and maintain contact with the defensive player.

C

D

THE CENTER

While the offensive guards and tackles need to be able to execute all of the blocks described above, the center has to be able to execute them after snapping the ball to the quarterback—a difficult task.

The center's stance is the same as that of the other offensive linemen except that at least one hand must be grasping the ball in preparation for the snap to the quarterback. Some centers put both hands on the ball. Others cradle the free arm over the left knee. Still others place the free hand on the ground since they feel it gives them better balance.

It is of paramount importance that the center charge as he snaps the ball. A common error is to snap the ball and then charge. Since the defense can

The Center's Stance

Both hands on the ball.

One hand on the ball, one hand free.

charge as the ball is snapped, an immobile center can be overpowered by the defensive player, who will be moving forward.

The center snap can be executed best if the center concentrates on lifting the ball and charging over it rather than snapping back to the quarterback.

As the center charges, he must be able to execute all of the blocks described for down linemen, though he rarely needs to execute their trap or lead techniques. Most offenses do not have the center pull for a wide run or lead for a trap because of the possibility of a collision with the quarterback right after the snap.

The exchange of the ball between the center and the quarterback must be automatic. The snap must be quick and clean. The center lifts the ball naturally into the hands of the quarterback. There must never be any bobble or fumble.

One hand on the ball, one hand on the ground.

Blocks of the Center

The Running-Play Block

A

B

C

The Pass Block
The techniques of both blocks are the same as for any down linemen, but to execute them effectively, a center must charge his opponent as he snaps the ball.

A

B

C

THE TIGHT END

The tight end must be able to execute all of the blocking techniques of offensive guards and tackles. In addition, he should be capable of running pass routes and catching the football well. The ideal tight end is tall and strong, but agile.

Play of the Tight End

The tight end's stance is the same as the three-point stance described for down linemen. But it is also important for the tight end to be able to get off the line to become a pass receiver. There are two basic moves to avoid being held up on the line of scrimmage by a defensive player—fake a block or use a head-and-shoulder fake to draw the defensive man out of position.

Faking a Block

A   B

By making a genuine effort to block the opponent quickly (A,B), the tight end (dark jersey) entices the opponent to avoid the block (C), allowing the end to move down-field and become a pass receiver (D).

Faking a Block

On normal down and yardage situations, the defensive man playing over the tight end is never certain whether the end will block him on a running play or attempt to get downfield to catch a pass. In faking the block, the tight end should, as the ball is snapped, drive his shoulder into the belt buckle of his opponent. He then follows through on the block, attempting to turn the defender either to the right or the left as described for the one-on-one shoulder block for down linemen. *The end should make a genuine effort to block the opponent quickly.* This will entice the opponent to avoid the block—get out of the way of the blocker—which will then allow the end to move downfield to become a pass receiver.

C

D

The Head-and-Shoulder Fake

A   B

In this sequence, the tight end fakes to his left to get off the line of scrimmage. He starts in the three-point stance, head up, with eyes straight ahead so as not to give away his move (A). At the snap he steps left with his left foot and simultaneously

The Head-and-Shoulder Fake

On long yardage situations, the defensive player over the tight end will ignore the fake shoulder block technique since he knows a pass play is much more likely than a running play. Even if the end does try to block him for a run, he can retreat, avoid the block and tackle the ballcarrier before enough yardage is made for a first down.

The defender's sole purpose on long yardage situations is to hit the tight end on the line of scrimmage and keep him from getting downfield. To avoid being held up, the end should take a quick step with his left foot and move his shoulders and head to his left side. As the opponent reacts to this movement, the end should push strongly off his right foot back to the inside to get past his opponent. This fake can be used to the opposite side as well.

Running Pass Patterns

Once the tight end has gotten past the defender, either by faking a block or using the head fake, he moves downfield to become a pass receiver. He then uses the techniques described for wide receivers in the following chapter.

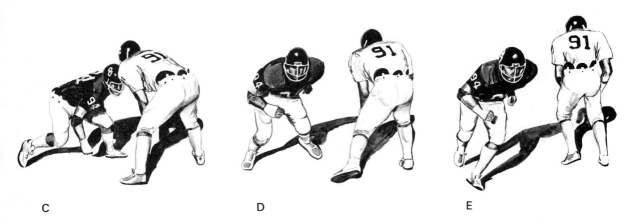

C   D   E

moves his head and right shoulder to the left (B), faking his man in that direction. Now he shifts his weight quickly to the right, stepping forward with his right foot (C,D). On his very next step (with his left foot), he is gone, free to receive a pass (E).

SUMMARY

The play of the offensive line determines the success of the offensive team. Great pass receivers will never have an opportunity to catch the ball unless the offensive linemen protect the passer so well that the quarterback has time to throw without worrying about the rush of the defense. Likewise, great running backs will have no chance to use their skills unless their offensive linemen control the line of scrimmage and effectively block their opponents. Players like Jim Brown and O. J. Simpson would seem to be ordinary ballcarriers unless their linemen had blocked effectively enough to get them started downfield to use their strength, speed, and deceptive running techniques.

Unless a ballcarrier can be unimpeded until he is three to five yards beyond the line of scrimmage, he will have little chance to use his skills. To this point on any play, running backs appear to be of the same ability. It is when the superior ballcarrier has moved three to five yards downfield—thanks to the blocking of his offensive line—that he can use his great skills to make a long gain or a touchdown.

Seldom do the offensive linemen get their deserved recognition. The run-

Solid blocking by the offensive line is the heart of any team's offense.

ning backs, the passers, and the receivers always get the lion's share of public attention. Their opportunity to use their skills, however, depends on the effective blocking of their offensive linemen. This illustrates the fact that football is a total "team game." The men who rarely receive their fair share of publicity and acclaim actually are the most needed element for a successful offense.

5

Techniques of the Wide Receivers

The most dramatic change in recent years in offensive football has been the ever-increasing ability of passers and receivers to move the ball with the passing attack.

The hot-stove argument as to who was the best quarterback of all time—Sammy Baugh, Johnny Unitas, Joe Namath, or Joe Theisman (the list could be far longer)—will never be resolved. But no one disputes that today a college or professional team must have an effective passer.

A few years ago, most teams practicing their pass offense would work with the quarterback and receivers against a skeleton secondary of linebackers and defensive backs. In the session, rarely would the passer be able to complete more than 60 percent of his throws. Today, passers have improved to the point that in the skeleton drills it is not unusual to have 90 to 95 percent of the throws completed. In games, today's college and professional quarterbacks must be able to complete more than 50 percent of their passes if their team is to win.

The skill of receivers has improved just as much. Tight ends like Kellen Winslow are strong blockers and have great running speed and faking ability. Wide receivers like Cliff Branch and Roy

57

Speed, finesse, and sure hands are the marks of outstanding wide receivers.

Green possess burning speed, great aptitude at catching the ball, and the ability to run precise pass patterns.

Since so many of today's players possess these skills, offensive formations have been changed to exploit more carefully the potential of their passers and receivers.

A novel use of a wide receiver was a key part of Coach Earl Blaik's West Point teams in the late 1950s. Football then was a one-platoon game, which was

The Wide Receiver's Stances

The Sprinter's Stance

The Erect Stance

much more physically demanding. To eliminate the need for the wide receiver to be in the huddle and then run out to his position, Coach Blaik had his wide receiver stay wide and not go to the huddle each play. The man received the signal for the play to be run via hand signals from his tackle, in much the same way baseball coaches on third base signal to the batter. This maneuver led sportswriters to christen Bob Carpenter, Army's wide receiver, the "Lonely End."

A few years ago, the standard passing formation had one wide receiver to either side of the field. This spread the defense and forced the defensive team to cover the field from sideline to sideline.

Today it is relatively common to have three wide receivers, and the trend seems to be toward using four wide receivers much of the time, as the Washington Redskins have done.

Wide receivers should use one of two stances: a sprinter's stance or an erect stance. In either case, the wide receiver should look to his inside to watch the center snap the ball. Because of his distance from the quarterback and the usual crowd noise, it is hard for him to hear the snap count, so he must watch to be able to move as the ball is snapped.

BLOCKS OF THE WIDE RECEIVERS

While the wide receivers are primarily potential pass targets, they should be able to block well. It is comparatively easy for these men to get good blocking position, but timing the block is extremely difficult because they are usually so far ahead of the ballcarrier. When the ballcarrier is only two steps behind the blocker, almost any contact by the blocker on the defensive player will make it easy for the runner to get past the opponent. But if the block is made 10 yards or more ahead of the ball, even a defensive player who is knocked to the ground can often recover, get up, and make the tackle. Thus, the wide receiver must time his block to hit the opponent when the ballcarrier is close to them.

The two types of blocks used by the wide receiver are the *pick-off block* above the waist of a lineman or linebacker moving from the inside out to cover a wide play run to the side of the wide receiver, and the *downfield block* after the receiver has faked running a deep pass route. Maintaining position on the defender is the key to both blocks.

A   B

The Pick-Off Block
The blocker cuts in (usually from the outside) at an angle to the defensive man (A)
and makes the block with his shoulder (B).

GETTING OFF THE LINE OF SCRIMMAGE

It is for their pass patterns that wide receivers are famed. First, though, the receiver must get off the line of scrimmage. Defensive players will attempt to keep him from getting downfield by knocking him down at or near the line of scrimmage. If the defense plays a man on the receiver on the line of scrimmage, the receiver must be able to evade him to get downfield.

Just before the snap of the ball, the receiver should look at all defensive players in his area. If a man is on him or close to him, he should assume that this man will attempt to knock him down. As the ball is snapped, the receiver starts downfield, watching only the defensive player closest to him. The receiver can avoid the defender in a variety of ways. He can move quickly to his inside or his outside and then reverse direction to cut past the defender. Or, if the defender is playing the receiver on the line of scrimmage, the receiver can take one step, make a sharp head fake to either side and then reverse direction to move past the defender. If the defender does not take the first fake, the receiver can go past him on the original course.

The rule here, as in all phases of the game, is to use the eyes alertly. If the receiver takes his eyes off his opponent, the defender can hit him when he is not poised for it and knock him down. By seeing only the defender and faking properly as described, the receiver can get off the line of scrimmage and past the defender. Now he is in position to run his route to catch the ball.

Different signal systems for the pass patterns to be run are used by different teams. The most-used system is the "pass tree," which tells the receiver which route he will run on each play. There will be subtle refinements in the route to be run but the "pass tree" tells the receiver his basic pass route.

On odd numbers the receiver will break to his left at different depths downfield. On even numbers he will break to his right at different depths downfield.

On Route 1, the receiver breaks to his left after going 6 yards downfield. On Route 3, he breaks out at 12 yards; Route 5 at 18 yards; Route 7 at 25 yards; and on Route 9 he runs a pattern aimed at the flag that marks the juncture of the sideline and the goal line.

On Route 2, the receiver goes downfield 6 yards and breaks to his right. On Route 4, he breaks right at 12 yards; on Route 6 he breaks right at 18 yards;

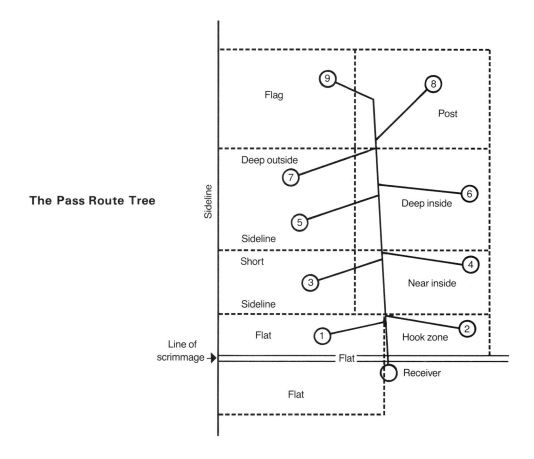

The Pass Route Tree

and on Route 8 he breaks right at 25 yards and runs directly at the goal post.

Assuming that the team is using the pass tree numbering system, the three receivers (the split end, the tight end, and the flanker back) all run the same tree. The quarterback calls the pass pattern using 3 digits. The split end is usually the "X" man. The tight end is "Y" and the wide receiver is "Z".

For example, if the number 587 is called, the split end will break out at 18 yards, the tight end will run the 8 pattern to back the defensive safety out of the play; and the flanker back will run the 7 pattern, which should free him in front of the safety.

Pass Pattern 587

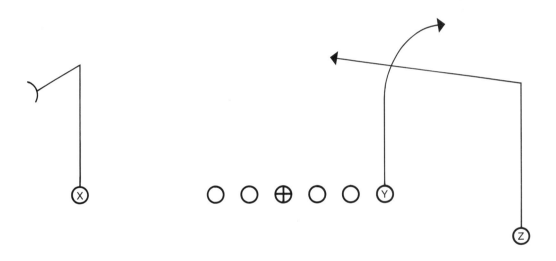

By using this signal system, an offensive team can run every conceivable pass pattern, but as noted above, each pattern must be refined to improve its effectiveness.

Some teams call their pass patterns by verbally describing the pattern to be run by each receiver. We will use the verbal description to describe the individual pass patterns.

Receivers run three different types of routes on pass plays: *individual patterns,* in which the receiver attempts to get open by his own fakes; *"combination" patterns,* in which he and a teammate combine their patterns to enable the primary receiver to get open; and *"play action" passes,* in which the fake of the running play lures the defensive secondary up to stop the run and thereby allows the receiver to get open.

Individual Patterns

Different terms are used by different teams to describe individual patterns, but these terms are generally descriptive of the patterns to be run.

The Slant Pattern

This route is designed to hit a receiver who is not being immediately covered by the defense. The pass should be thrown approximately one second after the ball has been snapped. The receiver moves at a 45-degree angle to the inside. He looks for the ball immediately. If a defender is playing in position to cut off the slant pattern, the quarterback should "check" signals at the line of scrimmage to another play.

The Slant Pattern

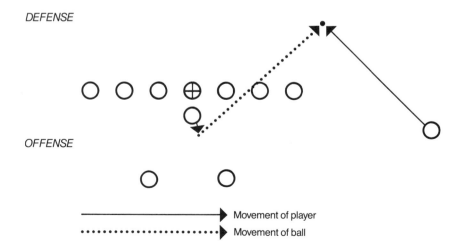

DEFENSE

OFFENSE

Movement of player
Movement of ball

The Hitch Pattern

This route should be used when the defender is playing deep off the line of scrimmage, fearing the receiver will have enough speed to get behind him. The receiver takes two steps downfield, then drops back a step while looking for the ball. If the defender is playing on the line of scrimmage or within a yard or two of the receiver, the quarterback should check signals.

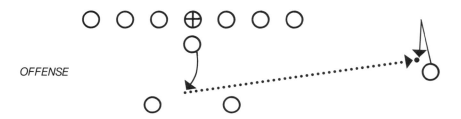

DEFENSE

The Hitch Pattern

OFFENSE

The Sideline Pattern

On this pattern the receiver breaks down the field as fast as possible and attempts to lure the defender into turning and running to keep the receiver from getting behind him. As the defender turns to run, the receiver plants his inside foot and breaks on a slight angle back and toward the sideline.

When this play is called on third down, the timing of the cut will depend

The Sideline Pattern

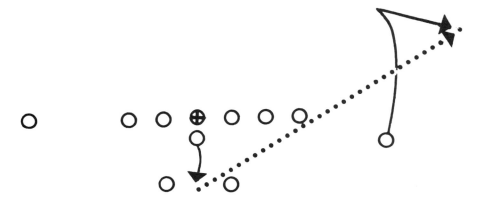

on the yardage needed on the play. For example, when the ball is on his own 35-yard line on third and 6, the receiver should break to go out of bounds about 7 yards beyond the line of scrimmage. If 12 yards are needed, the receiver should make his break to go out of bounds approximately 13 yards from the line of scrimmage.

The passer and receiver must practice the timing on the various depths of the cut so that the ball will be thrown just as the receiver plants his foot to begin his break to the outside. If the passer waits until the receiver has made his break, the receiver may run out of bounds before the ball reaches him or the defender may recover in time to block or even intercept the pass.

It is most important for the passer to throw the ball on a line only chest high at the receiver. This will enable the receiver to keep his torso and shoulders between the defender and the ball to protect it from the opponent as the catch is made, eliminating the chance of an interception.

The Curl or Hook Pattern

Here, the receiver goes off the line of scrimmage exactly as he does on the sideline cut. He drives downfield as fast as possible while keeping his body under control. He should drive for a spot about two yards outside the man covering him. This will force the defender to move to the outside. As the defender moves back and to the outside, the receiver curls to the inside, getting his back and shoulders between the defender and the flight of the ball. The curl should be made at the distance necessary to gain needed yardage on the play, as with the sideline cut. Again, the ball should be delivered to the receiver at chest height.

The Curl or Hook Pattern

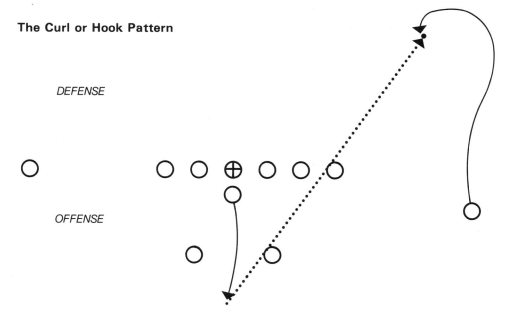

DEFENSE

OFFENSE

The Flag Pattern

On this pattern the receiver attempts to get behind the defender. He moves off the line of scrimmage in the normal manner, floats at about three-quarter speed while watching the defender, then breaks at full speed for the flag at the goal line on the sideline. The receiver should not look for the ball until he is past the defender and the ball has been thrown. This timing must be carefully worked out in practice. The quarterback should put the ball in the air about three or four seconds after it is snapped.

The Flag Pattern

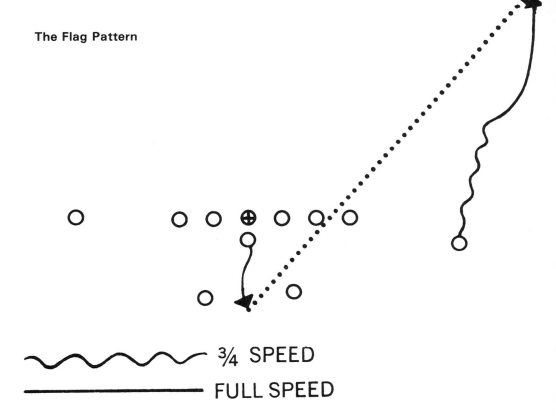

~~~ ¾ SPEED

——— FULL SPEED

The Post Pattern

In running this route, the receiver again comes off the line of scrimmage normally, floats as he did on the flag pattern, and then turns on the speed, running at an angle that will put him directly in the middle of the goalposts on the end line. He should not look for the ball until it is thrown, which will be approximately three or four seconds after the ball is snapped.

The Sideline-Flag Pattern

When the receiver is being covered closely by the defender on the sideline pattern, it is comparatively simple to get behind the defender by faking the sideline pattern and going deep. The receiver starts by running the sideline pattern. After making the break, he takes eight or ten steps on the sideline cut, being certain to keep his body under control. He then plants his outside foot and turns downfield, going full speed to run the flag pattern past the defender. The quarterback, too, must fake a pass in the sideline portion of the pattern, and he needs fine protection because the play takes time to develop. This play requires considerable practice but is beautiful to watch when executed well.

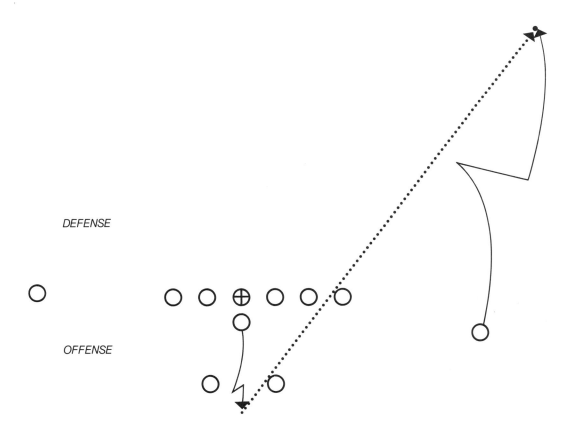

The Sideline-Flag Pattern

In this pass pattern, the quarterback fakes a throw and then, when the receiver breaks to the sideline, he resets and throws deep.

The Sideline-Flag-Sideline Pattern

Here, the receiver combines the sideline-flag pattern with a second sideline cut. He runs the sideline pattern, breaks downfield and then, after moving 6 to 8 yards, he again plants the inside foot and runs a second sideline cut. It is almost impossible for the defender to cover this pattern. But since it takes a relatively long time to run the pattern properly, the pass protection must be exceptional if the passer is to have time to fake a pass once or twice and then throw the ball.

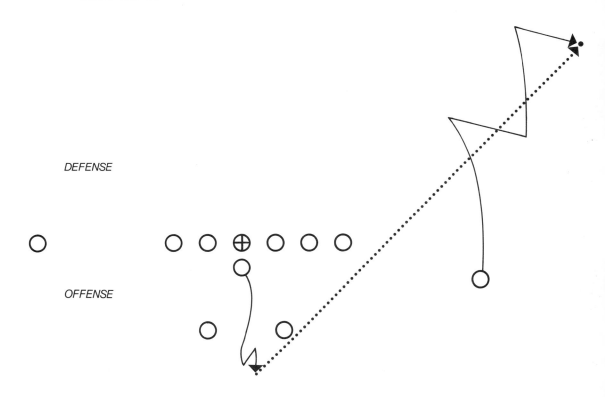

The Sideline-Flag-Sideline Pattern
As in the sideline-flag pattern, the quarterback fakes a throw and then, when the receiver breaks to the sideline the second time, he resets and throws deep.

The Curl-Sideline Pattern

On this pattern the receiver runs the curl pattern to the inside, then plants his inside foot and breaks on a sideline pattern to the outside. Again, a fake by the quarterback helps free the receiver.

A wide variety of routes can be developed from the basic patterns just described.

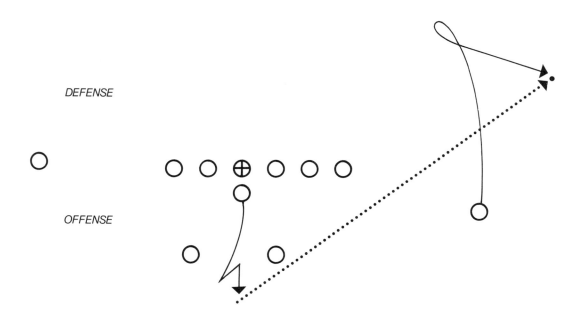

The Curl-Sideline Pattern

The quarterback fakes a throw and then, when the receiver pivots and breaks to the sideline, he resets and throws deep.

Combination Patterns

Combination patterns between two receivers to open one man are likewise designated by descriptive terms: "flanker-flag tight-end-out," "split-end-curl halfback-flag," or "ends-cross". There are many other combination patterns, but the following should help illustrate the theory.

"Flanker-Flag Tight-End-Out" Pattern

The flanker runs the flag route to take the defensive man back deep and thus clear the flat area for the tight end who will break to the flat about four yards deep.

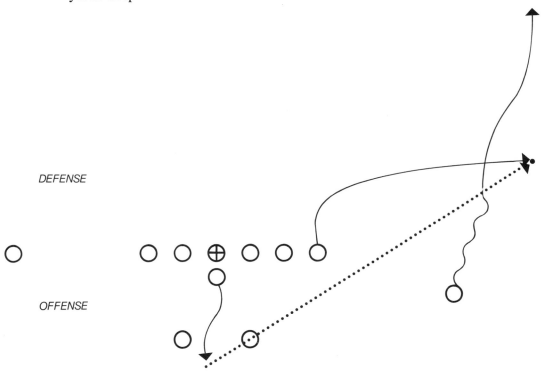

The "Flanker-Flag Tight-End-Out" Pattern
The flanker runs the flag route (see page 66) to take the defensive man back deep and thus clear the flat area for the tight end who will break to the flat about four yards deep.

"Split-End-Curl Halfback-Flag" Pattern

The split end runs his regular curl route. As he makes the curl, the quarterback pumps and fakes a throw to him to draw the defensive halfback up to cover the curl. The halfback floats out of the backfield, running low to conceal, if possible, his movement. As the end curls, he breaks deep at full speed on the flag route, attempting to get behind the defensive halfback. The quarterback resets and throws deep to the offensive halfback.

The "Split-End Curl Halfback-Flag" Pattern

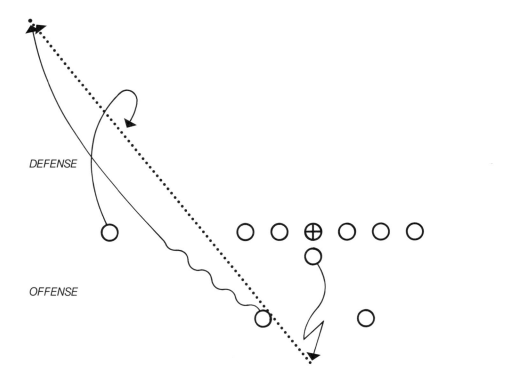

"Ends-Cross" Pattern

The split end drives at the outside leg of the defensive halfback to "widen" him slightly. Eight yards from the line of scrimmage, he breaks straight down the field to take his opponent deep. The tight end clears the line of scrimmage and watches the defensive halfback on the far side. As that man moves back to cover the split end, the tight end breaks full speed for the open area in front of the defensive halfback.

The "Ends-Cross" Pattern

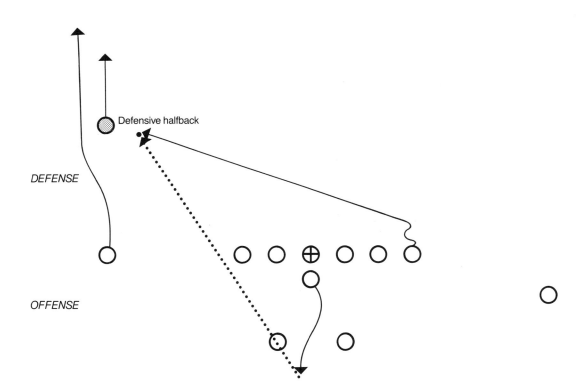

Defensive halfback

DEFENSE

OFFENSE

Play-Action Passes

Getting the receiver open on a play-action pass depends on the ballhandling and faking of the quarterback and the running back.

It is possible to run an effective pass play from the set-up for almost every running play. This tactic helps the running attack, since the defensive secondary men cannot "support" against the run until they are *positive* the play is *not* a pass. The following is one example:

The Toss-Trap Pass

As the ball is snapped, the quarterback fakes a quick toss to the "flaring" halfback and then makes a careful fake to the halfback hitting in on the inside play. After completing the fake he moves slowly back to his passing position. Meanwhile, the tight end moves downfield on a sharp inside angle, as if he were positioning himself to block the safety on the trap. As the safety moves up to stop the faked trap, the end breaks past him on the post pattern.

The Toss-Trap Pass

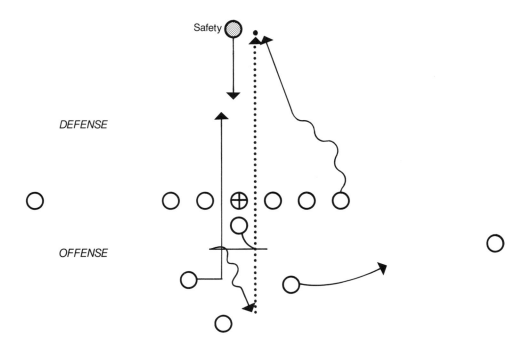

HOW TO CATCH THE BALL

Catching the ball requires disciplined use of the hands and eyes. Two common errors prevent players from becoming capable receivers:

- *Looking for the ball too soon.* Until the ball is in the air, on many plays the receiver may be considered a potential blocker whom defenders are at liberty to hit and knock down. To avoid this, the receiver should watch the movements of the defensive players in his area and not turn to look for the ball until he knows the quarterback is ready for release.

  Different pass plays have a variety of ball-delivery timings. The longer the ball is in the air, the longer the receiver can delay in looking for it. The quarterback and the receiver should practice together on "count passes." For instance, the quarterback may deliver the ball at the count of five. The receiver goes down the field, making whatever fakes fit the pass route to be run, and makes the final break at the count of

Looking the ball into the hands

Wrong

Right

five before he turns to look for the ball, knowing that it will soon be on its way.

- *Taking his eyes off the ball just before it reaches him.* The receiver's failure to "look the ball into the hands" can cause him to miss the pass. The temptation to take your eyes off the ball is understandable since you see the ball on its way and know you can make the catch. Instinctively you want to look at possible defenders who may be closing in on you to make the tackle. But if you take your eyes off the ball you won't be able to make the catch because you have broken the hand-eye coordination necessary to receive the ball properly.
- A receiver who concentrates on watching the ball can make miraculous, acrobatic catches. A receiver who breaks this fundamental rule can muff an easy pass. Remember, a football, because of its shape and size, is not as easy to catch as a baseball.
- The hands must be in a soft, relaxed position at the time the catch is made, ready to cradle the ball and draw it toward the body.

The position of the hands when catching the ball

Wrong

Right

• The receiver should run the pass route, using his hands and arms to lend balance and add speed to his running, not raising them to catch the ball until it is close. Reaching for the ball too soon puts the receiver off balance, tensing the hands and arms and making the catch more difficult.

Never reach for the ball too soon!

Wrong

Right

Drills

Here are two drills that quickly improve the ability of pass receivers:

· The receiver should start from about three yards to the left of the coach who will toss the ball to him. He runs straight ahead at half speed. The ball is tossed softly a distance of about eight or ten yards. The receiver catches the ball onehanded with his left hand. Repeat the drill with the coach tossing the ball from about three yards to the receiver's left, so that he catches the ball onehanded with the right hand. He will quickly learn the proper way to cradle the ball as it is caught. The drill also helps to develop good hand-eye coordination, since he must watch the ball carefully to catch and hold it with one hand.

· This is a drill to teach the receiver to "see" the ball into his hands. The coach should write numerals in chalk or ink on both ends of the ball on each of its four panels and ask the receiver to run the regular pass patterns and call out the number on the ball at the moment he catches it.

The "See-the-Ball-into-the Hands" Drill

Paint numerals on both ends of the ball and ask the receiver to call out the number on the ball at the moment he catches it.

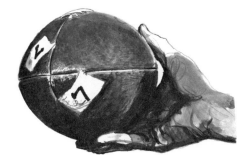

Running Backs

Great running backs come in various styles and sizes. They have different proportions of power and speed and elusiveness. No one as fast as Herschel Walker is as strong as he is. No one as elusive as O. J. Simpson was as fast as he was. No one as big as John Riggins is as fast.

But all great running backs share certain characteristics: quickness, balance, agility, and the ability to change directions without losing speed. The psychological requirements are equally important. The running back usually is the defensive team's principal target. Defensive players focus all of their physical toughness not only on stopping him on an individual running play but also on seeking to intimidate him, punish him, wear him down.

Great running backs can resist this onslaught because they retain a deep commitment to scoring a touchdown every single time they carry the ball. With that commitment, the back will always fight for extra yardage by making a determined second, third, and fourth effort to stay on his feet and move toward the goal, rather than surrendering to the first hit.

79

Great running backs, like Eric Dickerson, are fast, elusive, and strong.

BLOCKING

The effectiveness of his teammates' blocking skill is the major factor that helps determine yardage gain. But the running back must also have blocking skills. By blocking well for the other backs, he improves his team's morale tremendously. If he is a prima donna and does not block effectively, a deterioration in team attitude often takes place, and eventually the other offensive players will not block for him as well as they could. Every running back should work to improve his own blocking capability so that his teammates will respect him as an all-around player.

Running backs need to execute four types of blocks: *blocking a man out, blocking a man in, taking a man either way with an "isolation" block* and *blocking to protect the passer.* The key to all blocks is: *Get the proper position on the opponent, and maintain contact.*

Blocking an Opponent Out

To block the opponent out effectively, the back must get his *inside foot* closer to the line of scrimmage than the opponent's. Once he's in this position,

Blocking an opponent out
The key to blocking an opponent out is getting the inside foot closer to the line of scrimmage than the opponent's.

the block becomes simply the regular shoulder block. The back should expect to make the toughest possible charge as the ball is snapped—which means to come down the line of scrimmage from the outside to the inside without getting any depth across the line of scrimmage. To counter this, when the ball is snapped, the back moves at such an angle that he can meet his opponent at the "crossroads" and still have his inside foot closer to the line of scrimmage than the defensive man's. As he moves, he should watch his opponent intently. If the defender makes a normal charge across the line of scrimmage slightly to the inside, the blocking back can adjust his course as soon as he has gained inside-out position. As he reaches the area of impact, he should have a good base, be in the hitting position, and deliver the block with a sharp thrust of the back, shoulders, and legs. The target remains the same—the opponent's belt buckle.

Blocking an Opponent In

The hook-in block is much like the scramble block described for linemen. Again, the back expects the defender to move on a course that will make the block as difficult as possible. This would be to come softly straight across the line of scrimmage ready to give ground to the outside. To make the play, the blocker must get his outside foot *beyond* the outside foot of the defender.

To block a man in while moving to the right, the blocker moves straight for the sidelines from his original position, watching his opponent. He *must* remain deeper than the opponent. If the opponent crosses the line rapidly and is approaching a point deeper than the blocker, the blocker must give ground to remain deeper than the defender. As the blocker approaches the area of contact, he should be in the hitting position. He must stay on his feet and get his right foot farther to the outside than either foot of the defender. As this position is reached, he swings his left arm with the uppercut motion, getting the elbow and upper arm beyond the thigh and hip of the opponent. He then follows through with his left thigh, hooking the opponent by driving off the right leg.

If the defensive man is determined to get deeper across the line of scrimmage than the blocker, the blocker should let him get a yard deeper and position himself for the regular hook-in block. But then, driving off his right foot, he should swing his hips and legs to the right and make a "reverse body block," knocking the opponent down. The block will be made so deep across the line of scrimmage that the ballcarrier can run his regular course even though he goes inside the defensive man.

Blocking an opponent in
Here, the key is getting the outside foot beyond the outside foot of the defender.

As the ball is snapped, the blocker must watch the opponent. If the defensive player does not make the difficult charge but instead moves to the inside and does not attempt to get much depth into the backfield, the blocker will adjust his course to put himself in position to execute the block as described.

Hooking a man in while moving to the left is done exactly the same way, except that it is the left foot that must be outside the defender at the moment the block is made.

The Isolation Block

The isolation block is used against a lineman or linebacker left exposed by double-team blocks of the linemen, which usually open a big hole at the line of scrimmage. The back's objective is to take on his opponent squarely and let the ball carrier "run for daylight" to either side of the block. Again, the essential is to make and *keep contact*.

As the ball is snapped, the blocker moves directly at his opponent, keeping his eyes on the belt buckle. As he approaches the area of contact, he should be in a low hitting position and have enough momentum to overpower the defender. If the blocker is moving with force and intensity, the defender must go around the blocker to get at the ballcarrier. As he commits himself to one side or the other, the blocker adjusts to hit with the proper shoulder to make and keep contact. The ballcarrier watches the defensive player and adjusts his course to go to the side *opposite* the move of the defender.

The Pass-Protection Block

The pass-protection block is used to defend an area. The blocker knows where the quarterback will set up to throw, and his purpose is to keep the defensive man from penetrating to that spot. Since the defensive pass-rushers will use a variety of patterns, the blocker does not know which man he will block until the defensive player arrives in his area.

As the ball is snapped, the blocker moves to the spot where he will protect the quarterback. As pass-rushers move forward, he watches intently to pick the man coming into his area. Current rules enable the blocker to use his hands against the pass-rusher. He makes the block as described for offensive linemen, using a blow with his hands to turn the defender out and around the spot from which the quarterback will throw. He should make and maintain contact as he rolls his man to the outside.

If the rusher flattens his charge so that the blocker cannot use his hands to force him to the outside, he should turn the defender to the inside and take him past the throwing lane.

RECEIVING THE BALL

The ballcarrier gets the ball one of two ways: a hand-off from the quarterback or a toss from the quarterback. On the hand-off, the running back is moving with maximum speed and the quarterback must delicately place the ball on the back's outside hip. The quarterback should think of the ball as being a hollow eggshell, so that he will softly hand it to the running back instead of slapping it against the hip.

Correct hand and arm position when receiving the hand-off is vital. The outside hand should be curled in slightly, just inside the hip, to block the ball if the quarterback extends it too far. The inside elbow should be up, with the forearm parallel to the ground, opening the target—the outside hip—for the

Preparing to Take the Hand-Off

Right   Wrong

quarterback. The runner should make sure he does not keep the inside elbow too low, blocking the ball.

A good ballcarrier takes the hand-off from feel, watching only the defensive players in the area he will hit. If he looks for the ball, he'll lose sight of the defense and miss the holes. By keeping his eyes focused on the area to be attacked, he can react to the movements of the defensive players and cut accordingly.

When the ballcarrier feels the ball being placed on his far hip, he drops his inside elbow over the ball and cradles it with both hands and arms. Dropping his inside elbow over the ball protects it if he is hit during the hand-off. If the blocking is effective and he breaks past the line of scrimmage, he can grasp the ball with either hand and move it to the proper carrying position.

When the ball is tossed to the running back on a pitchout, he must "look it into his hands" while running as fast as possible. Just as in pass receiving, taking the eyes off the ball is disasterous.

Fumbles—devastating in their effect on the offense—will seldom occur if the quarterback and ballcarriers painstakingly practice hand-offs and pitchouts.

Taking the Hand-Off

The receiver takes the hand-off while watching the defensive players in the area he will hit.

CARRYING THE BALL

The ball must be carried properly. Television announcers are forever accusing running backs of carrying the ball like a loaf of bread, and carelessness in that basic duty of the runner *does* cause countless fumbles. One point of the ball should rest in the palm of the ballcarrier's hand, with the opposite end tucked underneath the elbow. That protects both points of the ball, preventing a tackler from hooking it away, causing a fumble. A common mistake is to expose the point of the ball by having the thumb and forefinger wrapped around the end of the ball rather than protecting the point with the palm of the hand. Exposing the ball this way makes it far easier for a defensive man to jolt or pry the ball loose.

In open-field running, the hand and arm carrying the ball can be moved away from the body to aid the carrier's balance and thus his speed. If he is in imminent danger of being tackled, however, the runner should bring the ball in tight against his rib cage, to protect it.

Proper ballcarrying position

WATCHING THE DEFENSIVE MAN

Coaches debate whether it is better for the running back to watch his own blockers or to watch the defensive men. While watching the blockers seems logical, it is actually much better to watch the defensive man. The blocker will be attempting to knock him to one side or the other. If the runner expects the block to be successful but the defensive player beats the blocker, he will be tackled. If he watches the *defensive man,* however, he will always be able to break to the proper side.

The ability to run for daylight is the running back's most important skill. Great runners like Tony Dorsett, Eric Dickerson, and John Riggins are not necessarily built alike, but they each possess the uncanny ability to watch and read the defense, find the hole, and accelerate through it.

All great ballcarriers have the ability to accelerate beyond their normal running speed. Gale Sayers was an outstanding example. Apparently running full speed, he always had an additional burst of speed in reserve. This extra speed is the quality that separates the great from the ordinary runners.

Watching the Defensive Man

A

The ballcarrier watches the defensive man to see which side he will protect (A).
The defender protects to his right: the ballcarrier breaks the opposite way (B).
The defender protects to his left: the ballcarrier breaks to the right (C).

B

C

FAKING WITHOUT THE BALL

The most difficult fundamental for the running back to execute consistently well is to *fake carrying the ball.* If the defenders believe the man has the ball, they'll go all out to hit him. If the faking back immediately shows the defense

Faking Without the Ball

In faking to get the ball, the runner puts his hands and arms in the same position as he would to get the ball in a hand-off, and the quarterback puts the ball into the far hip (A).

The runner drops his inside elbow as if to cover the ball as the quarterback pulls it back out. The player then fakes running with the ball (B).

that he doesn't have the ball, he won't be hit nearly as hard. And since it is instinctive to avoid being hit, faking consistently well requires intensity of purpose.

The runner should curl to the inside upfield to hide the quarterback from the defense. In faking to get the ball, the runner puts his hands and arms in the same position as he would to get the ball in a hand-off, and the quarterback puts the ball into the far hip before withdrawing it. By grasping both elbows with both hands, the running back will appear to have the ball. Using the same elusiveness as he would if he had the ball, he should continue running until tackled, or until the play is over.

RUNNING WITH THE BALL

Speed, elusiveness, and power are the basic qualities of the great ballcarrier. Most of these are natural attributes: He was born with the needed abilities and has sharpened his skills through constant practice.

Basic ballcarrying techniques can be learned—the stiff arm, the crossover step, the fadeaway step—and ordinary running backs can improve their ball-carrying skills by practicing these basic techniques.

The Stiff Arm

This fundamental requires the ballcarrier to extend his arm with the elbow locked while he places his hand on the helmet of the would-be tackler. The ballcarrier pushes off the helmet and swings his body away from the defender. The best way to practice this technique is to have a teammate hold a blocking dummy. The ballcarrier moves forward at the dummy, extends his arm, and pushes off the dummy as he moves his body away from the dummy. If he is making the stiff arm with his left arm, he swings his body to his right, and vice versa.

If a blocking dummy is not available, the ballcarrier should practice the technique as described above against a teammate who is in a crouched set position. Constant repetition using both the right and left arms will greatly improve the stiff-arm technique.

The stiff arm
Note how the ballcarrier's elbow is locked as he pushes himself away from the
defender.

The Crossover Step

The crossover step can be used in conjunction with the stiff arm. Often,
however, in heavy traffic the ballcarrier lacks the time and space to use the stiff
arm effectively. If that is the case, the ballcarrier, when in the area of the
would-be tackler, swings his inside leg with a powerful thrust to get him past
the tackler. The inside foot must hit the ground before the outside foot.

Again, this technique can be practiced with the stiff arm as described above
or without the stiff arm as the ballcarrier moves past a dummy or a teammate
who is posing as a tackler. This technique should be practiced using both the
left and right leg as the crossover leg.

The Fadeaway Step

The ballcarrier plants his inside foot on the ground. Then, as his outside
foot hits the ground, he swings his inside leg back and to the outside away from
the tackler. As that foot hits the ground, the ballcarrier steps further to the

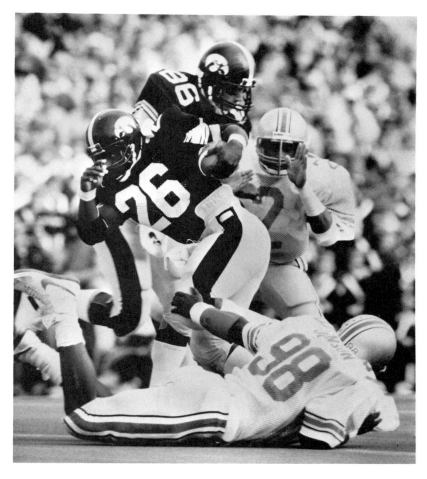

Specialized steps, such as the fadeaway and the crossover (shown here), help make running backs more elusive.

outside with his outside foot, fading away from the defender, and continues down the field.

This technique can be executed with the stiff arm or against a teammate posing as the tackler. The ballcarrier should practice the fadeaway step with both his left and right legs.

As noted, great running backs instinctively execute these fundamental skills. Ordinary runners, however, by practicing these techniques, will greatly improve their elusiveness and ballcarrying ability.

7

The Quarterback

The quarterback is the key player on the offensive team. Since he initiates every play, his skills contribute to the success of every play. The quarterback's duties are twofold: He must execute each play with mechanical perfection and, in addition, must lead the team and set the offensive strategy by his play selection. Many coaches reduce the second responsibility of the quarterback by calling all plays from the sidelines. Whether or not the quarterback calls audibles, however, his leadership is important to the offense and to the team.

Being relieved of play-calling enables the quarterback to concentrate on mechanical execution. But when a play is called from the sidelines by a coach, a particular defensive alignment is assumed. If the defense uses a different pattern, it may be strong against the play called. At this point the quarterback should check signals to change the play. If he is capable of doing this and calling a play that avoids running against that strong alignment, he is probably capable of total play selection without help from the sidelines.

93

What makes a quarterback like Joe Montana great? Intelligence, poise, leadership, self-confidence—and solid technique.

"The offensive play actually begins when the quarterback enters the huddle. . . ."

THE STARTING COUNT

The offensive play actually begins when the quarterback enters the huddle. He *should not* enter until the rest of the players are in position. By waiting, he lessens the possibility of getting bad advice from his teammates. While the huddle forms, he should ascertain the down and yardage situation and the lateral and vertical field position of the ball and decide on the next play. He then joins the huddle and takes command of the team. He calls the formation, play, and snap count with confidence, his voice and bearing dominating his men.

Having called the signals, the quarterback commands, "Break." The team moves to the line of scrimmage and sets up in the formation called. The quarterback positions himself behind the center, ready for the snap. He analyzes the defense to be certain that the play called has a reasonable chance of success. If not, he should check signals.

The quarterback's voice must be loud and clear when he calls the starting count or checks signals, since the team *must hear the signals* if they are to respond properly. The quarterback should call the snap count in a staccato tone so that the players develop a rhythm and break together to attack.

As the starting count is called, the center snaps the ball to the quarterback.

Proper Exchange

A proper exchange allows the quarterback to set up for a pass or hand-off in one fluid motion.

Poor Exchange

In this example, the quarterback is standing too upright (A), a common problem with young quarterbacks. He then takes his first backward step too soon (B). Result: fumble (C).

The quarterback's hands are placed under the center's crotch and turned about 30 degrees to the left. The thumbs of the hands are together, the fingers are spread naturally with the right forefinger in the middle of the center's crotch, touching with enough pressure so that the center can feel the location of the quarterback's hands, which must remain there until the ball reaches them.

The normal rotation of the ball as the center's arm and hand swing up and back will place the laces of the ball across the fingers of the quarterback's throwing hand. This gives him the "fat" of the ball and enables him to throw or hand the ball to another back without rotating it.

The center and the quarterback should practice constantly until the exchange becomes automatic. The handback must be executed as fast as possible and be absolutely foolproof. No fumbles!

Upon receiving the ball at the snap, the quarterback grasps it with his fingers over the laces to give him the proper "feel" and control of the ball.

THE HAND-OFF

In making a hand-off, the quarterback knows which back will get the ball and where in the backfield. As soon as the quarterback has the ball, his eyes should focus on the far hip of his runner. Concentration on this small target requires discipline. The tendency of an inexperienced quarterback is to be overly aware of the defense and see the running back only as a blurred object. By focusing on the proper small target, he will be able to place the ball delicately on the far hip. If he can't reach that hip, he should keep the ball to avoid a fumble. Ironically, when the quarterback does miss the hand-off and keeps the ball, the play often succeeds because the running back expects to get the ball and will make an excellent fake, running with maximum power in the expectation of being the ballcarrier.

After handing the ball off, the quarterback must *never* let his eyes follow the ballcarrier. Instead, he should carry out the continuing play fake.

By focusing on the running back's outside hip, the quarterback executes a perfect hand-off to him.

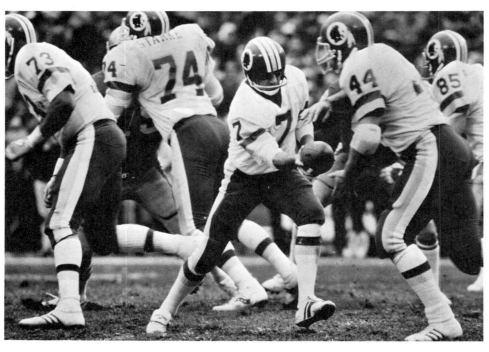

FAKING A HAND-OFF

In faking the hand-off, the quarterback must use his eyes to mislead the defense. All of us are curious by nature. We tend to look at whatever anyone else is staring at. Similarly, the defense will tend to commit itself toward whatever back the quarterback looks at.

When he is actually going to hand the ball off, the quarterback must move to the ballcarrier. When the quarterback is to fake giving the ball, the ball carrier must come to the quarterback.

When faking the hand-off, the quarterback should hold the fat of the ball in both hands, quickly reaching out with it to hit the stomach of the faking back and then riding the ball with the faking back as he hits toward the line of scrimmage. As the back clears the quarterback, the quarterback should pull the ball back and place it on his own hip while following the faking back with an empty hand and a hard stare. This must be done in a firm, confident manner so that the defense believes that the faking back has the ball. The quarterback must not rush his next move: He should give the defense ample time to take the fake.

Here, the quarterback fakes and keeps the ball, hiding it on the hip away from the line.

THE QUARTERBACK OPTION PLAY

The varied use of the quarterback option is the most significant offensive development in college football in recent years. In its pure form the quarterback simply runs at the defensive end with a trailing back approximately 5 yards deeper than the quarterback. If the end moves in to tackle the quarterback, the quarterback tosses the ball back to the trailing halfback. If the end crosses the line deep to protect against the possible pitch, the quarterback keeps the ball and turns upfield. The play is easy to execute if the quarterback concentrates on one thing: *Watch the defensive end.* Whatever the end does will be wrong.

The quarterback holds the ball approximately chest high, balancing it in both hands but controlling it with the right hand when moving to the right, and with the left hand when moving to the left. He should move at the end with as much speed as possible while still maintaining the balance necessary to make a right-angle turn upfield if the end crosses the line to protect against the pitch.

As the quarterback angles toward the line of scrimmage, he should be sure to gain ground. By doing this, he pressures the defensive end to commit himself to stopping him or letting him keep the ball. While moving on this course the quarterback intently watches the end, ready to play it either way, depending on the movement of the end. If the end gets deeper than he is, the quarterback immediately plants his outside foot and turns upfield to run for daylight. If the end stays on the line of scrimmage and moves toward him, the quarterback simply flips the ball with the control hand in a soft, high pass to the trailing back.

The pass should be thrown shoulder-high so that the trailing back can catch it easily while running full speed without losing momentum. A low pitch may cause him to stumble or fumble, or slow him up.

When the quarterback keeps the ball, he must operate as effectively as possible as a ballcarrier. The fundamentals involved here are the same as those for running backs.

The Quarterback Option Play

He pitches.

A

B

The Quarterback Option Play (Cont.)

He keeps the ball.

A

B

In modern offensive football the quarterback must be able to throw forward passes consistently well. The defense is pressured by not knowing whether the play will be a pass or a run. If the quarterback is *not* a skillful passer, the defense can gamble that he won't be able to complete a pass, even to a receiver who is left open.

The quarterback should be able to throw both from a standing set position for drop-back passes and on the run. The running pass puts great pressure on the defense. If they drop back to cover the pass, the quarterback can run with the ball. If the defense commits to stop the threatened run, he can throw the ball to an open receiver.

The Drop-Back Pass

Since it is easier to throw the ball from a set position than while running, most coaches base their pass attack on the drop-back pass. The quarterback must move to the passing position for the designated play as quickly as possible. His drop can be done in two ways. If the quarterback is a gifted athlete, he can drop straight back while facing the line of scrimmage, enabling him to watch the movement of the defense the entire time. If he can't run backward fast enough without losing balance, it may be necessary for him to turn and run back to his set position while looking over his shoulder at the defensive team.

The depth to which the quarterback drops depends on the pass pattern and timing of the play being run. The quarterback has three basic drops—the three-step drop, the five-step drop, and the seven-step drop.

On three-step drop plays, the ball should be delivered within two seconds. On these passes the wide receivers will run a quick "out" or "in" pattern, or the tight end may run a quick "slant" pattern.

On the five-step drop, the quarterback will throw the ball 3 or 3½ seconds after the snap. Receivers can run the individual patterns described for wide receivers or any of the "combination" patterns.

On the seven-step drop, the ball should be delivered in about 4½ seconds. Wide receivers will be attempting to get behind the defensive secondary or

The Five-Step Drop

Upon receiving the snap from the center, the quarterback twists his body so that he can scan the field for his receivers while running back five steps. Note the position of the ball during the drop-back: near the quarterback's shoulder.

A

B

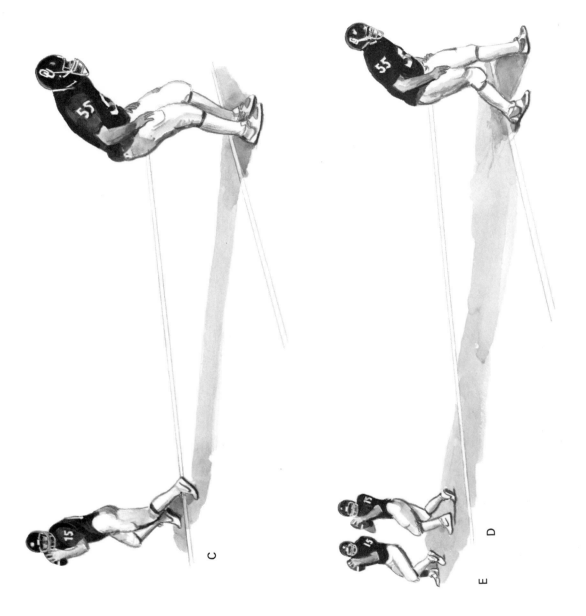

C

D

E

The Drop-Back Pass

A

The right-handed quarter-back steps with his left foot exactly in the direction he will throw the ball (A).

B   C

At the same time, he cocks the ball behind his right ear, holding it with his fingers across the laces (B,C).

running a "combination" pattern across the field 15 to 18 yards from the line of scrimmage. Also, running backs who are not needed in pass protection may move out of the backfield to become "secondary" receivers.

Except for the three-step drop, the quarterback should not look at his primary receiver since he knows precisely where he will go. By looking only at the receiver, he will not be conscious of the position of the defense and an interception may result. Instead, the quarterback should watch the play of the linebackers and defensive secondary and then throw to the open receiver.

In preparing to pass, the quarterback should have the ball in both hands approximately shoulder-high. When ready to throw, he steps forward with his

D

In delivering the ball, he lets it rotate off the palm of the hand to the fingertips to give it a spiral motion (D).

E

He follows through like a baseball pitcher, his throwing hand shoulder-high, palm facing the ground (E).

F

Follow-through, front view (F).

left foot (assuming he is righthanded) in the exact direction he will throw the ball, and at the same time he cocks the ball behind his right ear, holding it with his fingers across the laces. In delivering the ball he lets it rotate off the palm of his hand to the fingertips in order to give it a spiral motion. He then follows through in the same manner as a baseball pitcher. After he has released the ball, his throwing hand should be shoulder-high with the palm facing the ground.

The quarterback should learn to throw three types of passes: a fast clothesline pass; an arched ball over the linebackers and in front of the defensive secondary; and a long, deep throw downfield to a receiver who is getting behind all defensive secondary men.

The Running Pass

The delivery of the ball on the running pass is performed in the same way as on the drop-back pass. Since the thrower will be running at practically full speed, however, additional techniques must be learned.

The righthanded passer will not have much trouble throwing the ball while moving to his right. But when moving to his left, he must twist his upper body against the momentum of his run, which makes it virtually impossible to throw the ball hard or with accuracy.

The Running Pass

When the right-handed quarterback runs left, he is forced to throw against the momentum of his body: not an easy way to pass.

The key to throwing well on the run is to be moving *toward the line of*
scrimmage at the time the ball is delivered. Then the passer's momentum aids
the delivery of the ball. Again, the passer should read *the defensive man*
covering the primary receiver instead of looking at the receiver.

A

B

By turning toward the line of scrimmage as he delivers the ball, the passer adds
valuable body momentum to his pass.

The Miami Dolphins' Dan Marino can adjust his play to any situation.

BROKEN PLAYS

One of the most recent adjustments in the passing game is the execution of the "broken play." It usually appears to spectators that on a broken play when the quarterback is scrambling, he is freelancing and is plain lucky to find a receiver open. In modern football, the opposite is true.

When a pass play is called, whether it be a three-step, five-step, or seven-step drop, the receivers know when the ball should be thrown. If the ball is not thrown when expected, the receivers run a predetermined second course in an attempt to get open. The good quarterback, while scrambling, knows exactly what second pattern all receivers are running. Consequently, he knows where his receivers will be after the primary pattern has broken down.

Well-coached offensive passing teams spend 40 to 45 percent of their practice time on the so-called broken plays. Thus there really should be no broken plays. When the timing of the regular pass pattern has not succeeded in getting a man open, by using his mobility while scrambling, the quarterback executes a predetermined second play while his receivers are running new, adjusted pass routes.

This is another example of adjusting the point of attack *after* the ball is snapped, so important to offensive football.

Effective offensive formations are those that allow the offense to attack the entire defense. On the line of scrimmage, the quarterback has the option of running the prearranged play or calling a new play in response to the defensive alignment.

Basic Offensive Formations

A wide variety of offensive formations are used in modern football, but each must have the same fundamental plays that enable the set to attack the entire defensive team. Regardless of the formation being used, the team must have plays that:

- Hit inside.
- Hit wide.
- Use faking and "misdirection" to fool the defense.
- Feature play-action passes.
- Use the pass-run option, in which the ball-carrier can run or throw, depending on the reaction of the defense.

Prior to World War II, the two popular offensive formations were the Single Wing and the T. The best college teams of the era, Minnesota and Pittsburgh, both used the Single Wing, as did the Washington Redskins of the National Football League. Their great quarterback, Sammy Baugh, was, in fact, a Single Wing tailback for the Skins before the war.

Earlier, Notre Dame, under the legendary Knute Rockne, used the T formation as their opening offensive set. The Irish ran about one out of every six plays from the T. To keep the defense off-balance, the rest of the time they shifted from the T to their version of the Single Wing—the Notre Dame Box. This use of the T formation created a double problem for the defensive team. They were never sure whether a play would be run from the T—or whether the offensive backfield would shift to the Box set, which then required the defensive team to move to the side where the backs shifted.

The shift was executed by six men. When shifting to the right, both ends moved out one yard away from their tackles, making it easier for them to get downfield on a pass or improving their blocking angle. The right halfback moved up and stationed himself as a wingback just outside his offensive end. The fullback moved over and lined up behind the offensive tackle. The quarterback moved over and lined up between the offensive guard and tackle. The

The Notre Dame T Formation, before the shift.

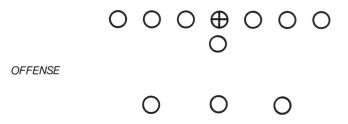

The Notre Dame shift from the T to the Box Set (Single Wing).

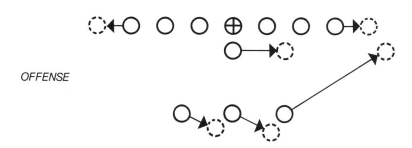

other halfback moved over and lined up directly behind the center. The movement of these six men made the formation very strong to the side shifted. This required the defense to move to that side in order to present a balanced alignment against the new formation.

The shift could be executed either to the left or to the right. Thus, the defensive team was forced to be ready to defend against a play run from the T formation, and then be ready to adjust their alignment either to the left or the right as the ends and backs shifted.

When Rockne first used this tactic, the rules did not require the offensive team to remain solidly set for a one-second count. The first couple of years the tactic was used, Notre Dame was so successful that the football rules committee changed the rule and required that every offensive player remain motionless for a count of one second before the ball could be snapped. This new rule gave the defense time to move to its new alignment and be reasonably ready to defend as the ball was snapped.

The T formation, as we know it today, was first used by Stanford University under Clark Shaugnessy in the middle 1940s. During the war, he became the advisory coach under Dud DeGroot of the Washington Redskins. The 'Skins were so successful offensively that the other pro teams almost immediately changed their offense from the Single Wing to the T. George Halas and his Chicago Bears dominated the National Football League for a number of years using the T under their star quarterback, Sid Luckman.

As noted above, before World War II, the Single Wing was the most popular offensive formation. After the war, more and more teams went to the T formation or variations of it with the quarterback directly behind the center and in position to get the ball on an instantaneous snap.

Few teams today use the Single Wing formation. This is a result of timing as it relates to the reaction of the defensive team. When a play starts from the T formation, the ball almost instantly is in the hands of the quarterback who can pass it, pitch it, or hand it off.

THE T FORMATION

The basic T formation is perfectly balanced. It can quickly hit every inside spot along the line of scrimmage, and it allows great deception since any of the three backs may get the ball. This is not a strong passing formation, however, because no receivers are detached wide.

The quick timing of the center's snap to the quarterback—in contrast to the Single Wing center having to throw the ball back to the fullback or the tailback—was the fundamental factor that caused most coaches to change their basic offense from the Single Wing to the T.

In recent years, offensive formations have become far more open through the increased use of wide receivers—flankers and split ends—which forces the defense to cover the field from sideline to sideline on every snap. When teams use a compact formation like the Single Wing or the straight T, the defense can surround the formation reasonably well since it covers only about 45 feet of the 160-foot width of the field. Consistent passing from compact sets is difficult because all the receivers are close together when the ball is snapped. With detached men, all possible receivers are already separated by great distances, which puts additional pressure on the defensive team.

It should be noted, however, that unless the offensive team has a strong-armed quarterback who can deliver the ball accurately with reasonable range, it is a waste of time, and poor strategy, to detach receivers. The defense can ignore them since the quarterback will not be able to throw the ball to them anyway.

The need to spread the defense has led almost all teams to play with at least one detached receiver, and the vast majority of teams use two. The free substitution rule has made it possible to play as receivers men who possess tremendous speed but who may not have the physical qualities required for other positions. They learn to run routes with great deception because they devote almost all of their practice time to perfecting their receiving skills.

On all formations, the interior line is the same. The center, guards, and tackles take their positions with no variations except a slight adjustment in the distances between offensive linemen. The Split-T attack is based on changing the splits between linemen, but the major formation changes result from the placement of the offensive backs and ends.

THE SINGLE WING

In the Single Wing, the ball must be thrown back from the center to the fullback or the tailback. While the ball is in flight, the defense knows exactly where it is. This gives the defensive linemen a chance to hit and control their opponents while they still know the exact location of the ball. The time it takes the ball to get from the center to the back is short, but the defensive players moving with the snap of the ball have time to start controlling their opponents before the pattern of play has formed.

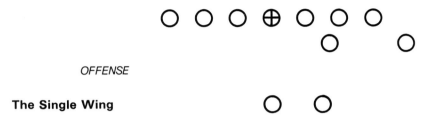

DEFENSE

OFFENSE

The Single Wing

THE OPEN SET

Popularized by the professional teams, the Open formation consists of a split end and a flankerback, with one tight end and two running backs. The running backs usually take their position about four yards behind the offensive tackles, but their positions vary depending on the play. The Open Set has these advantages:

- · It is perfectly balanced to either side.
- · It makes the pass play a constant threat since there is a wide receiver out to each side.
- · It provides for balanced running since either running back can hit quickly straight ahead or off-tackle.

The major weakness of the Open Set is its inability to generate power inside. With only two running backs in the formation, it is difficult to hit quickly and still have a back leading inside plays.

The Open Set

OFFENSE

◯
Split end

◯ ◯ ⊕ ◯ ◯
◯

◯
Tight end

Quarterback

DEFENSE

◯
Flanker back

◯
Running back

◯
Running back

THE TWIN SET

Both wide receivers are on the same side of the field, opposite the tight end, in the Twin Set. This pattern puts pressure on the defense because the two most effective receivers can closely coordinate their pass routes and use each other to free one man.

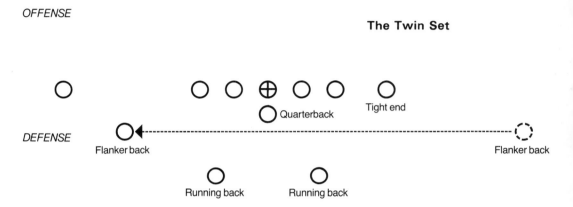

THE ONE-BACK SET

When a team has fine receivers, one strong running back, and a powerful offensive line, the One-Back Set becomes a sound formation. To cover all of the potential receivers, the defensive secondary and linebackers are spread across the field. There is little quick support available against running plays. If the offensive line can control the line of scrimmage, the remaining back can hit

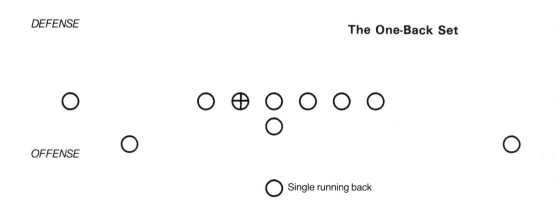

anywhere across the offensive front and use his power and strength behind the wall of his blocking linemen to pick up four or five yards consistently.

This set has been popularized by the Washington Redskins, who have the talented players to execute it to perfection.

THE SHOTGUN SET

Whenever the quarterback is directly behind the center to be handed the ball, it is difficult to protect him as a passer if the defense shoots men through every gap between the offensive linemen.

The only way the quarterback can be protected is to move the two remaining backs up where they can pick up rushers coming through the gaps on either side of the center. When this adjustment is made, the offensive team cannot execute its basic running attack and is committed to the pass.

The Shotgun set

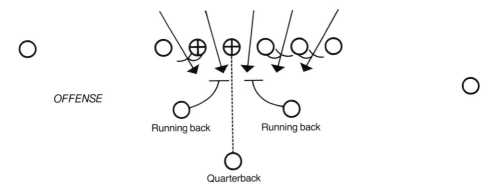

The running backs are in position to pick up
(block) the blitzing linemen.

To combat this defensive plan, on long-yardage, sure-pass situations, many teams now use the Shotgun formation.

In the Shotgun set, the quarterback takes his position six yards behind the line of scrimmage and the center snaps the ball back to him. The quarterback is already in position to throw and is protected against any type of rush since his backs can pick up the extra defensive men attempting to get to the passer.

A

B

The Position of the Quarterback in the Shotgun set
The quarterback stands six yards behind the line of scrimmage for the snap (A). Upon receiving the ball, he is instantly in position to throw (B).

The I formation is the same as the Open Set except that the running backs are positioned differently. The fullback is in a three-point stance about 3½ yards from the line of scrimmage. The tailback stands erect about 5½ yards from the line of scrimmage so that he can see the defense over his fullback all of the time.

This formation generates a powerful inside running attack since the fullback is in position to lead the tailback on running plays, or to hit inside quickly when he is the ballcarrier. It retains the same passing strength as the Open Set.

The I formation
The running backs become fullback and tailback.

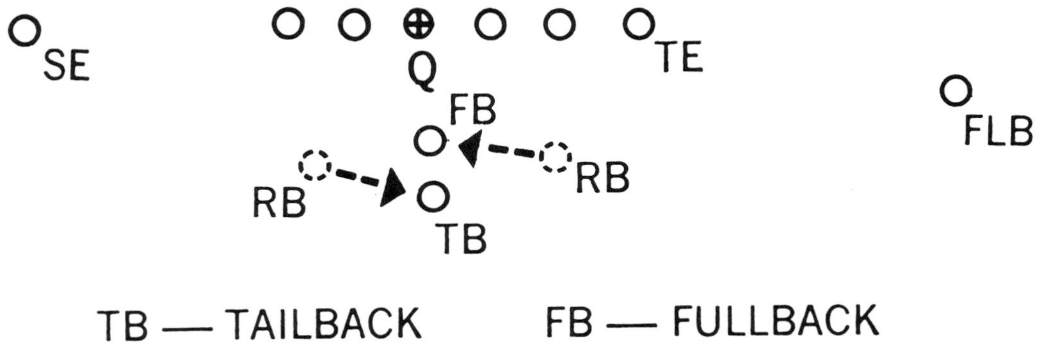

TB — TAILBACK   FB — FULLBACK

THE I SLOT

A common adjustment of the I formation is the I Slot. The flankerback becomes a split end and the tight end drops back into a wingback position about 1½ yards outside the offensive tackle and one yard deep in the backfield.

This formation has all backs in position to handle the ball on running plays, which adds tremendously to the number of offensive variations available. It also provides great deception on reverse plays, since the wingback can get the ball quickly after the quarterback has faked to the fullback or tailback.

The I Slot
The tight end drops back to become wingback; the flankerback moves up to become the split end.

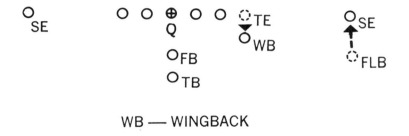

WB — WINGBACK

THE POWER I

Another variation of the I formation is the Power I, which is usually used in short-yardage situations or when a team is close to its opponent's goal line. It can be played with two tight ends or with one end split. The quarterback, fullback, and tailback are in the regular I position. The flankerback takes his position as a regular halfback, lined up about 3½ yards deep behind his own offensive tackle.

This formation has great power and great deception, since both the fullback and the halfback can lead to block on inside running plays. Any one of the three backs may end up with the ball after the quarterback has faked to one or two teammates.

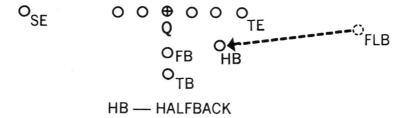

HB — HALFBACK

The Power I
The flankerback moves in to become a halfback.

THE VEER FORMATION

The Veer was originated by Bill Yoeman, coach of the University of Houston. It was the first of the so-called "triple-option" formations, but it retains two wide receivers so that the passing game is not limited.

On this set, the two running backs are lined up shading the outside of the offensive guards. As the triple option begins, one of the running backs hits over his offensive tackle and the quarterback places the ball on his far hip as he reads the defensive tackle. If the tackle crosses the line of scrimmage, the quarterback lets the running back have the ball. If the defensive tackle closes to stop the running back, the quarterback keeps the ball and moves out to option the defensive end.

The Veer formation in action

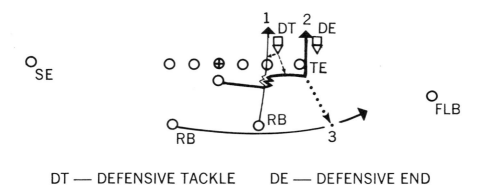

DT — DEFENSIVE TACKLE   DE — DEFENSIVE END

THE WISHBONE FORMATION

The Wishbone attack was pioneered by the University of Texas under its great coach Darrell Royal. The wishbone is a safer method of executing the triple option because the quarterback meshes with the fullback a yard and a half farther from the defensive tackle than is possible for the Veer triple option. This gives the quarterback a longer time to read the play of the defensive tackle. The quarterback reads the charge of the defensive tackle exactly as he would from the Veer triple option. If the defensive tackle crosses the line of scrimmage, the quarterback gives the ball to his fullback. If the defensive tackle stays on the line to play the fullback, the quarterback keeps the ball and moves out to option the defensive end.

The Wishbone formation
A one-man change from the Veer formation triple option forms the Wishbone: The flankerback moves in to become the fullback.

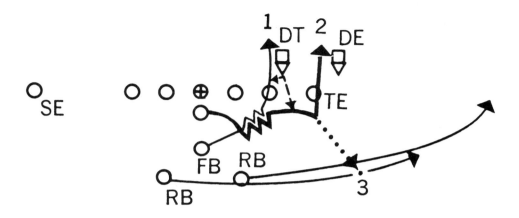

TEAM FUNDAMENTALS

The most important team fundamental is proper execution of the starting count. All the players must explode from the line at the same moment to get the jump on their opponents. An effective drill that takes little time or energy can develop this team skill: The players hold their hands about nine inches apart while the quarterback gives the starting count, says, "break", and then calls the snap signal. At the signal the players clap instead of charging. Scattered claps mean that they are not responding in unison—there should be only one clap heard.

Once in formation, all players must make certain to look straight ahead. Leaning by any offensive man will tip off the direction of the play. Looking at the point of attack can also be a giveaway.

Another fundamental of offense is to avoid errors. A consistently successful offensive team must not fumble, throw interceptions, incur penalties, or miss assignments. All of these errors can be kept to a minimum by a sound, sensible approach to planning the offense.

Offensive Team Fundamentals: What Not To Do

Body weight forward is a tip-off that the offensive man will charge straight ahead.

Body weight back is a tip-off that the offensive man will pull out or drop back to protect the passer.

The offensive player who leans and looks to his right tips off the direction of the play.

The player who leans and looks to his left also tips off the defense.

Defensive football has become increasingly sophisticated and complex.* Teams use a variety of defensive alignments. They change the angle of charge and stunt many ways from each defensive set. The defensive signalcaller is trying to outguess the offensive quarterback on every play.

This has necessitated development of new offensive tactics. Ascertaining the alignment of the defensive team before the snap is helpful. But since the defense will use a variety of charges and patterns from any alignment, the offensive team must be able to read these movements and adjust the point of attack *after the ball is snapped.* Both the Veer triple option and the Wishbone attack are based on these principles.

When the ball is snapped, the offense does not know whether it will be given to the faking back, kept by the quarterback, or pitched to the trailing halfback. The other plays used—the counter (where the QB fakes to one back and then passes the ball to another runner), the counter option and various play-action passes (where the QB fakes a running play, keeps the ball, is ready to throw it)—all start in exactly the same way as the triple option. Consequently, there is no "key" available to the defense to give it a quick tip as to the exact point of attack.

The same principle is essential to today's passing game. The so-called broken play explained above is simply a further exploitation of the adjustment of the offensive point of attack after the ball is snapped. The quarterback and receivers know when the ball should be thrown on all pass plays. When the ball is not thrown when expected, the quarterback has scrambled and moved out of the pocket. Receivers now run their new pattern, which has been carefully practiced. The quarterback, while scrambling, knows where all his receivers are and can pick out the open man and throw to him.

To repeat, in modern football, the defensive team will have a called play against the offense. Often they will completely cover the original point of attack of the offensive team whether the play is a pass or a run. To be successful, the offensive team must be able to adjust the point of attack on runs and passes *after* the ball has been snapped.

Ed. note: For a study of football defense, see *Sports Illustrated Football: Defense,* revised edition, by Bud Wilkinson (Harper & Row, 1986).

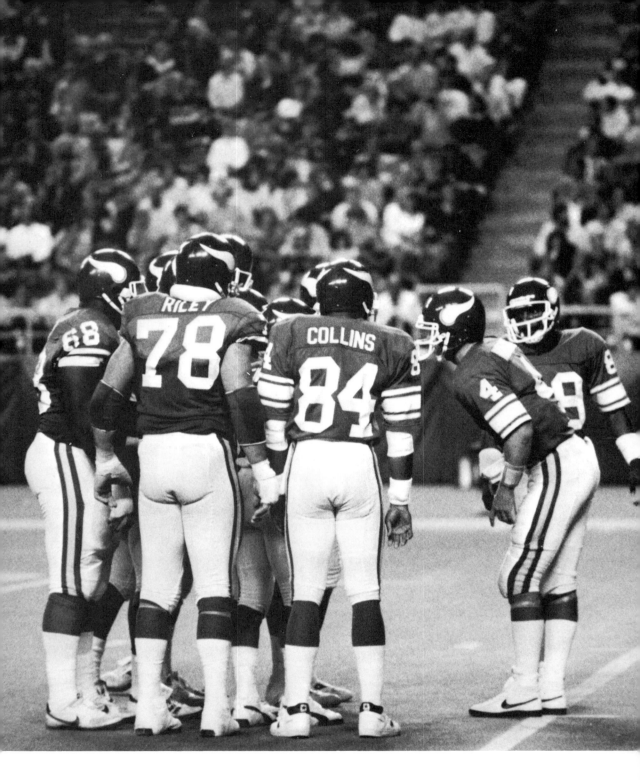

Quarterback Strategy

Sensible play selection is essential if the team is to maintain possession of the ball and score. A basic rule in quarterback strategy is: *Never try to force the issue with the defense.* Instead, hit its weakest area.

A key to calling the right play is field position.

In college and high school football, lateral field position can limit the offense. College hashmarks are one-third of the width of the field from the sidelines. Thus, when the ball is on the hashmark, the offense only has one-third of the field to the near sideline. Because it is difficult to get around the end to the narrow side of the field, many college defenses slightly overshift to the wide side of the field, the defense's area of greatest vulnerability. In professional football, the hashmarks are 70 feet 9 inches from each sideline. That gives ample room to run to either side of the field.

Vertical field position—the position of the ball relative to the defensive team's goal line—should always be a major consideration in play selection. Most coaches divide the field into four vertical zones.

In "the danger zone" it is essential to avoid a turnover through a fumble or interception. This

129

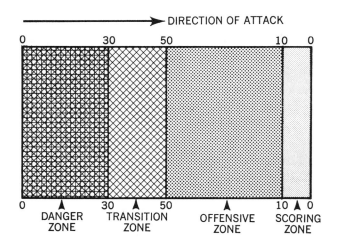

Quarterback's field plan

limits the number of offensive plays available to the quarterback. Don't gamble on any play that involves a high risk of a fumble or an interception: Either is likely to result in a field goal or a touchdown by the opponent.

In "the transition zone" the quarterback can be freer in the use of his total offense, but he still should not gamble with plays that have a high incidence of turnover.

In "the offensive zone" the quarterback can freely use his entire attack. He can gamble to make a first down to keep possession of the ball.

In "the scoring zone" the quarterback knows that he has four plays in which to score. He should plan all four before calling the first one. On first and second down, avoid calling plays that might result in any loss of yardage. On later downs, depending on the yards needed to score, go with plays that have the potential for longer gains.

When in the danger, transition, and offensive zones, the quarterback's first mission should be: *Make a first down.* This statement sounds obvious, but it isn't. If the quarterback hopes to score on one particular play—a long pass, for example—and isn't successful, the down has been wasted. But if he thinks in terms of making a first down and is repeatedly successful, it follows that he will eventually score. In addition, he will have maintained possession of the ball—and the team that maintains possession of the ball longest usually wins.

The quarterback must keep in mind that, until his team has possession of the ball deep in the opponent's territory, he has only *three* downs available to him, since his team will have to punt on fourth down. Whether the advantage stays with the offense or goes to the defense depends on the average gain the offense must make to earn a first down. By gaining 3 1/3 yards a play, an offensive team can make a steady succession of first downs. Although it is usually quite simple to make four yards on a play, it is difficult to make more than six yards.

For example, on "first and 10" the offense is relatively sure that it can make the first down if it does not lose yardage on badly executed plays or throw incomplete passes. A first-down incomplete pass is not particularly damaging to the offense: Only five yards per play are needed on the two succeeding downs to earn the first down. A five-yard loss on first down, however, means that the offense must average 7½ yards on the two succeeding downs to earn the first down. This is extremely difficult to do against a competent defense.

Except for scouting reports, the quarterback is pretty much in the dark the first time the offense has the ball. He knows the strengths of his own team and has some idea of the weaknesses of the defensive players as individuals, but, until the game begins, it's difficult for him to have a good feel of how things will go.

On first possession, the quarterback is seeking a play that will work. When he finds one that makes five yards or more, he has established the basis of his attack. The defensive weakness must be continually exploited, and he should repeat the successful play until the defense makes an adjustment to stop it. Actually, the quarterback should try to anticipate such an adjustment in time to avoid wasting a down. This ability to anticipate and change the play *before* the defense can stop it marks the difference between the great field general and the average signal-caller. There was probably no better model for this than Johnny Unitas.

It is axiomatic that the quarterback should call a play the defense doesn't expect:

- · If the defense expects an inside play, run wide.
- · If the defense expects a wide play, run inside.
- · If the defense expects a pass, run.
- · If the defense expects a run, pass.
- · If direct plays are not successful, use "misdirection" plays.

Marcus Allen's excellent moves as a running back allow him to adjust his point of attack to the play of the defensive team.

One can refine these statements into two fundamental rules of quarter-backing:

(1) The longer the yardage needed, the deeper the linebackers and secondary will play, making it easier to make substantial yardage inside.

(2) The shorter the yardage needed, the tighter the linebackers and secondary will play, making it easier to gain substantial yardage running wide or throwing.

As has been repeatedly stated, well-designed, modern football offenses are able to adjust the point of attack *after* the ball is snapped. This has alleviated the pressure on the quarterback's playcalling. In today's game, the fundamental choice is between a pass and a run. Both the pass and the run can be adjusted *after the ball is snapped* to the play of the defensive team.

An additional, simplified example of adjusting the point of attack is the use of the sweep play from the I formation. The quarterback tosses the ball to the tailback, who then is free to pick his hole as the defense adjusts to the play. He may execute a true sweep or may cut back anywhere inside. He may even reverse his field. A classic example of this play was Marcus Allen's Super Bowl touchdown run against Washington in 1984.

An effective offensive kicking game requires a coordinated offensive line.

10

The Offensive Kicking Game

The offensive kicking game has three phases—receiving kickoffs; punting the ball and covering the kick; and kicking field goals and covering the kick. (Points after touchdown are executed in the same way as field goals, but there is no need to cover the kick because the play ends after the attempt.)

RECEIVING KICKOFFS

The rules in high school and college football for receiving kickoffs differ from those in professional football. In high school and college games, five men on the receiving team must be lined up between their 45-yard line and the 50-yard line. In professional football, only three men are required to be in this zone.

High school and college rules-makers believe that the chance of injury on kickoffs is high because all of the players are usually running full speed at the point of contact. Requiring five men, instead of three, to be close to the kicking team limits the receiving team's ability to form a "wedge"—a moving triangular alignment in front of the returner—because the blockers must run back to get into position to do so. While they are going back, a kicking team can usually outrun them and prevent the formation of a true wedge.

In professional ball, the wedge is easily formed because two additional men can line up around the 30-yard line, where they can easily get in position for the wedge after the ball has been kicked.

The blocks on all kickoff returns must be properly timed in relation to the depth of the kickoff. The men on the receiving team should attempt to time their blocks to hit their opponents when the ballcarrier is about five yards from the offensive blockers. Blockers will drop further back on long kicks and less far on short kicks to time their blocks so they will not be too far ahead of the ballcarrier.

THE SIDELINE RETURN

On the sideline return, the man receiving the kickoff starts straight upfield so that he will not indicate too early whether the return will go to the left or the right. The blockers move to the outside of the men covering the kick and form a wall about 10 or 12 yards from the sidelines. After starting upfield, the ballcarrier moves to the side of his blockers and attempts to get around all the players and into the lane between the sidelines and the blockers. The blockers can use either a shoulder or body block. Their objective is to force their opponents to the inside to clear the return lane for the ballcarrier.

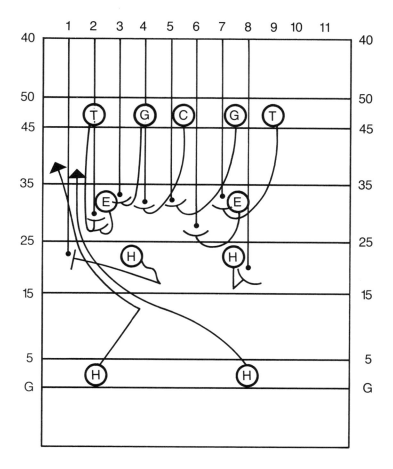

The sideline kickoff return

THE MIDDLE RETURN

The same fundamentals of timing on the blocks are used in the middle return as on the sideline return. Blockers hit their defensive men as shown in the diagram, and adjust how far they drop back to the length of the kick.

The middle return

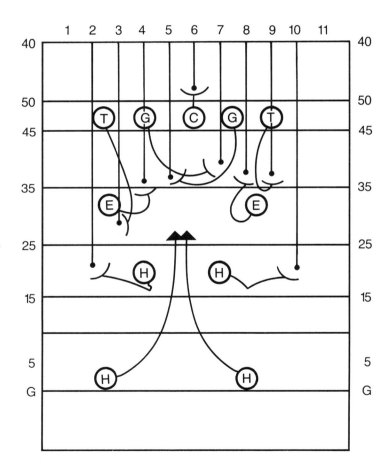

By delaying the covermen, the blockers need not adjust how far they drop back to the length of the kickoff. They execute pass-protection blocks and try to stop their opponents from getting further downfield than the 40-yard line. If they succeed, only the two outside covermen will be free to make the tackle.

Practically speaking, when this return is used, some of the defenders, after being delayed, will shrug off their blockers and close on the ballcarrier. But if he runs straight at the opponents' goal line—rather than laterally—he will usually be able to return the ball beyond his 30.

The delaying-the-kick-covermen return

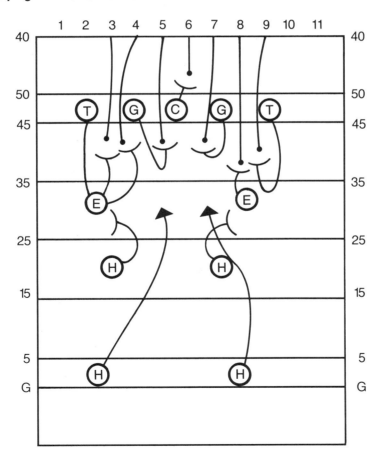

SPECIAL RETURNS

The receiving team's objective is always to get the ball beyond its own 25 or 30. A planned return executed with reasonable efficiency ensures that the play will put the ball in satisfactory field position. If the receiving team hopes to make a long gain or, possibly, a touchdown, it may gamble with a special return. There are two basic special returns. These are *the reverse kickoff return* and *the lateral pass return*.

The Reverse Kickoff Return

The reverse return is camouflaged by the course run by the man who catches the kick. He should start upfield and then break to the outside as he would if he were going to run the sideline return. The teammate to whom he will hand the ball must wait until the ballcarrier is almost to him before starting his own movement in the opposite direction. If he starts the reversing movement too soon, it will tip off to the covering team that a reverse is being run. The blockers drop back normally and then move to the side of the reverse. They use a body or shoulder block and establish the same wall of blockers as they would on a normal sideline return.

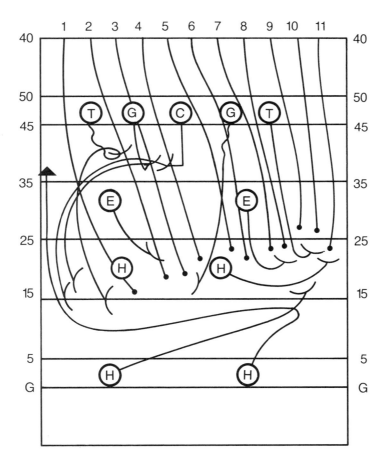

The reverse kickoff return

The Lateral Pass Return

On a lateral return, the man who will receive the pass fakes a block on his opponent and then drifts back to a position where he is *behind* the man who has received the kick and who will throw him the ball. As on all kickoff returns, the timing of the blocks and the throw of the ball will depend on how deep the ball is kicked. Again, the blockers use either a shoulder or body block as they set up their wall, just as on the sideline return.

The lateral pass return

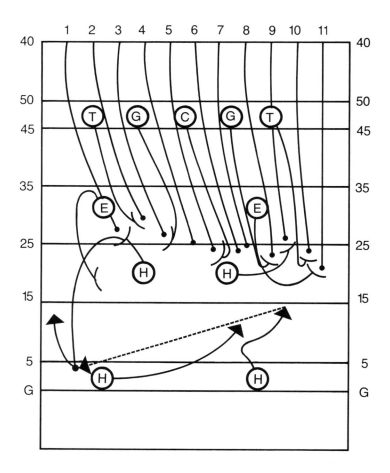

The problem with using the special play returns is the lack of assurance that the opponents will kick the ball to the desired man. If they make a "squib" kick or hit a line drive or kick the ball into the deep corner of the field, it is almost impossible for the receiving team to time the special plays properly. Scouting reports will indicate the power of the kicker and the direction in which he usually kicks. In most cases, though, the team can assume the ball will be booted straight down the field.

PUNTS

In the punting game, again, there is a difference between college and professional rules. In college football, all men on the kicking team are eligible to cover the kick as soon as the ball has been snapped. In professional football, only the two outside men—the men on the end of the line of scrimmage—can start to cover as soon as the ball is snapped. No other men on the punting team can cross the line of scrimmage until the ball has been kicked. The purpose of this rule is to make it easier for the receiving team to get a good return. The professional rules-makers believe that returns are exciting plays for the fans.

The most overlooked fundamental of the punting game is the importance of the center's long snap to the kicker, who lines up 13 to 15 yards from the line of scrimmage. The velocity of the center's snap is crucial to the success of the kick. The ball must be snapped fast and accurately. A bad snap makes the punter adjust his position and his hands to make the catch, delaying the kick and spoiling his kicking rhythm. It is important to note that the center—even if he cannot make a perfect snap—should always keep the ball low. That gives the punter a better chance to field the ball and get the kick away.

NET PUNT YARDAGE

In my opinion, statistics for punting should be changed. The length of the kick, statistically, is the distance the ball goes beyond the line of scrimmage. This ignores the 20-yard loss by the kicking team on a touchback if the ball goes into the end zone, and it overlooks the length of the return. Punting statistics would be fairer and more accurate if the 20 yards for kicking into the end zone and the length of the return were both subtracted from the length of the kick.

Although some individual punters, jealous of their statistics, might not like that change, it's important to remember that football is a team game. From a team's standpoint, the only important statistic on a punt is net yardage gained. Statistical purists have argued reasonably that a back who fumbles the ball should have 35 to 40 yards subtracted from his rushing yardage, since this is the distance the opponent can expect to punt the ball after recovering the fumble. The same thought could be applied to passers, with yardage subtracted from their total when they throw an interception. In spite of this logic, the current method of keeping statistics is unlikely to be changed.

HOW TO PUNT

The right-footed punter should take his stance with his feet slightly apart and his right foot slightly ahead of his left. As he catches the ball, he should take a short step forward with his right foot, then a full stride with his left foot as

How to Punt
The punter awaits the snap with his feet slightly spread, his right foot slightly forward, and his hands open to receive the ball (A). As he catches the ball (B), he takes

A   B   C

he drops the ball and then swings his foot forcefully into the ball.

The accuracy of the punter's drop of the ball is important. Since the punter is moving forward, he extends the ball at arm's length in front of himself as he drops it to coincide with the swing of his kicking foot. Before dropping the ball, the punter should rotate it so foot contact will be made on the side under the laces.

The punter should hit the ball on the outside of his instep. His foot should be turned slightly to the inside for maximum contact with the ball. He then follows through to put as much height and distance on the ball as is possible.

In learning to punt, players should first practice dropping the ball, making sure it strikes the proper part of the foot. No attempt should be made to punt for distance. The length of the kick should be only 15 to 20 yards.

After the punter has learned to hit the ball accurately, he can try to increase his punting distance gradually. He should never try to punt the ball as hard as he can until he has learned to drop it and hit it accurately with his foot.

a short step with his right foot (C), then a full step with his left foot as he drops the ball (D), and then swings his right foot forcefully into it (E). On follow-through, his right leg is fully extended and he is standing on the toes of his left foot (F).

D E F

Where the ball should strike the foot when punting.
Note the position of the laces
—away from the foot.

Good punters are keenly aware of the value of the net yardage gained on the punt. When the punter's range and field position of the ball would normally enable him to kick it into the end zone, he has two alternatives: Punt the ball out of bounds inside the 20-yard line, or make a "squib" kick. A touchback on a punt often represents a net gain of only 15 or so yards.

Unless the punter is extremely accurate, the squib kick is better than the attempt to punt the ball out of bounds. On the squib kick, the punter hangs the ball as high as possible in the air and gauges the distance so the ball will hit the ground on about the opponents' 10-yard line. The ball may be fair-caught there by the receiving team. If it is not, the punter's team can cover the punt and down it inside the 10.

PUNT PROTECTION AND COVERAGE

As in all football plays, a punt is a team effort. The team must first protect the punter and then cover the kick.

The center is in position to snap the ball. The guards split one yard away from the center. The two "up" backs line up one yard behind the line of scrimmage directly behind the split taken by the guards. The tackles line up one yard from the guards, and the ends line up as wide as they can, but must never split farther than a yard if there is more than one defensive man lined up to their inside.

Each of the blockers defends his zone and uses a pass-protection block against any opponent who attempts to charge through that zone. The fullback blocks the first man to get penetration from any spot along the line of scrimmage.

With each blocker defending his zone, a wall is established that protects the punter. If two defenders try to go through the same zone, they will be piled up by the one blocker defending that zone. After breaking the charge of any man attempting to rush the punt, all men cover the kick as rapidly as possible.

Punt protection

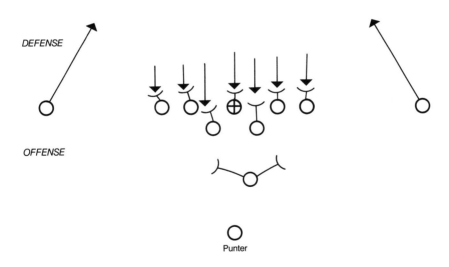

The two ends go directly at the man who is attempting to return the punt. They try to tackle the receiver aggressively as soon as he has caught the ball. The center covers straight downfield at the man who is in position to catch the punt. The guards widen out four to six yards from the center as they move downfield. The tackles widen out eight yards from the guards as they move downfield. By running these patterns, the punt cover team has put itself in position to move to the ballcarrier regardless of the type of return being run.

While the two ends go directly at the man who is attempting to catch the punt, the two tackles become what are known as the "turn-in men." It is their duty, if the ballcarrier breaks to the outside of the ends to either side, to turn the play back in. The center and guards adjust their course to put themselves in front of the returner. The fullback is the first safety. He does not cover the kick aggressively. As the ball is punted, he moves laterally to be in direct line with the man who receives the punt. He then covers carefully downfield to be in on the tackle should the returner get away from the ends or the second wave of blockers. The punter is the final safety man on the play. After kicking the ball, he moves laterally until he is directly in line with the man receiving the ball. He then stays directly in front of the returner so that he will be in position to make the tackle if the man has managed to break through the rest of the team.

Punt coverage

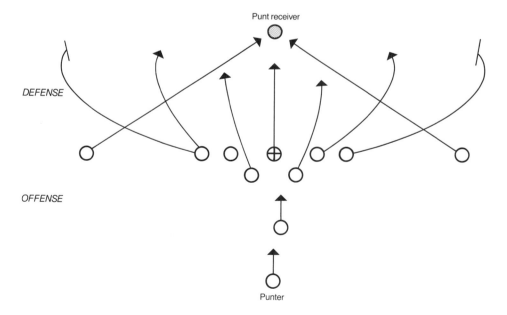

FAKE PUNT PLAYS

When the offensive team has the ball at midfield or closer to the opponent's goal line on fourth down and has to gain only two yards or less for a first down, the coach may elect to run an offensive play from punt formation rather than having his team kick the ball. When the offense goes to punt formation, the defensive team usually aligns itself to rush the kick or try to run a successful punt return. In either case, it is vulnerable to a well-executed play run from punt formation.

Running Play From Punt Formation

On a fake punt that's a run, the offensive team sets up in its regular punt formation. The right end starts downfield and then turns to his inside to block the linebacker. The defensive end usually comes across the line of scrimmage

Running play from punt formation
The punter fakes catching and kicking the ball.

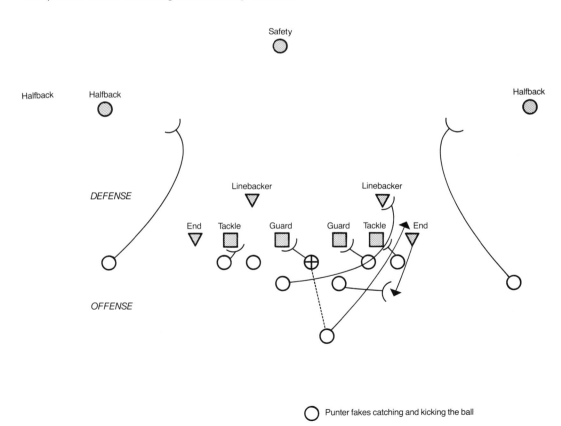

Punter fakes catching and kicking the ball

fast in an attempt to get in position to block the punt. The "up back" on the right side moves to his outside and blocks out the defensive end.

The right tackle, right guard, and center all block the opponents on their left. The left guard moves downfield and blocks the linebacker. The left tackle executes a scramble block on his tackle. The left end moves downfield as he would if he were actually covering a kick. The up back on the left side leads to his right and turns upfield just outside the right tackle's block and uses a shoulder block on the first opponent to come to him.

The punter, even though he will not receive the ball, fakes catching it and goes through his regular punting motion. This disguises the play and helps draw the defensive team into the patterns it usually takes in an attempt to block the kick.

But the ball is snapped to the fullback, who moves to his right and turns upfield inside the defensive end.

When the defensive team is expecting a punt and attacks the would-be kicker normally, it is vulnerable to the blocks described above. Usually, the fullback can make at least five yards on the play, and it is always possible that he may make a long run.

Pass Play From Punt Formation

To pass on a fake punt, the offense's right tackle, right guard, center, left guard, and left tackle all block their opponents to their left. Each end starts downfield as if he were covering a punt, but, when he is 10 or 12 yards downfield, breaks outside. The up back on the right side moves just outside the block of his right tackle and breaks into the flat zone approximately six yards beyond the line of scrimmage. The up back on the left side moves to his right and puts himself in position to block the linebacker if he rushes the punter. The fullback pauses momentarily and then moves to his right and uses a body block to take the defensive end to his inside. The punter catches the ball and takes the first two steps of his normal kicking motion. He then breaks to his right to get outside of the defensive end. The play now becomes a normal pass-run option. If the defensive halfback covers the end and the linebacker covers the up back, the punter will run the ball to gain the necessary yardage. If either the end or the up back is open, he will throw the ball to that man.

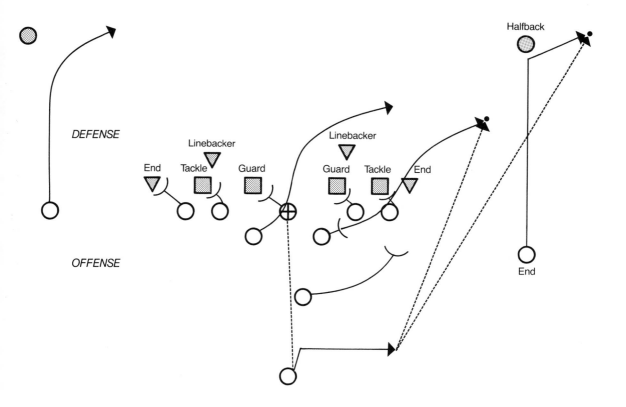

Safety

DEFENSE

Linebacker
Tackle

End

Linebacker
Guard

Guard   Tackle   End

OFFENSE

Halfback

End

Pass play from punt formation
The punter starts to fake the kick, but then runs to his right and throws to the end or the up back.

FIELD GOALS AND POINTS AFTER TOUCHDOWNS

In the 1920s and '30s, many teams used a dropkick for field goals and PATs. The ball, then, was shaped differently. It was quite rounded on each end and, when dropped, would usually bounce off the ground so that the kicker could boot the ball just after it came off the ground into the air.

As passing became more important as an offensive weapon, the rules-makers changed the shape of the football to make it easier for the passer to grasp it and throw it accurately. Today's ball is actually pointed at both ends. It is virtually impossible for a kicker to drop it so that it will bounce up where he wants it. This has virtually eliminated the dropkick from the game. Today, field goals and PATs are executed by having a holder catch the ball and place it in position to be kicked. This eliminates the problem a dropkicker would have if he expected a good bounce after dropping the ball.

Field goals and points after touchdown are executed in exactly the same way. The only difference is that the kicking team on a field-goal attempt must be ready to cover the kick to prevent the opponent from running the ball back, should the attempted field goal fall short or be blocked.

The placekicker on almost all college teams usually has enough length on his kicks to be able to make a field goal from his opponent's 30-yard line or even farther back if he has a truly powerful leg. Most professional teams have a placekicker who has enough leg strength to kick the ball over the opponent's goal post from their 40-yard line. Coaches are always trying to score points. When they have a good field-goal kicker and are within range, they usually will use the field goal on fourth down unless they have less than a yard or a yard and a half to gain. Coaches prefer to go for the "sure" three points rather than gambling on a fourth-down play to make the yards needed for a first down.

PROTECTING THE KICKER

The center takes his position to snap the ball back to the holder. The guards, tackles, and ends line up next to each other. As the ball is snapped, each man takes a short drop step back with his outside foot and positions himself to block any opponent who comes to his inside or from directly in front. The two "wingbacks" line up one yard behind the line of scrimmage just outside of their offensive ends. As the ball is snapped, each wingback takes a short step forward with his inside foot. The wingbacks must block any man who attempts to shoot

Protecting the field-goal (and PAT) kicker

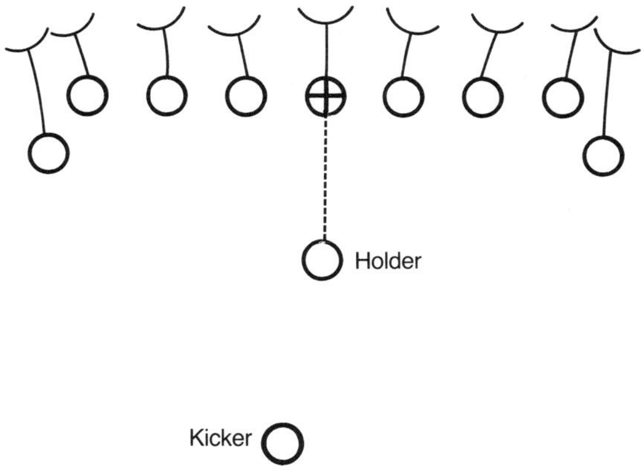

Holder

Kicker

Covering a field-goal attempt

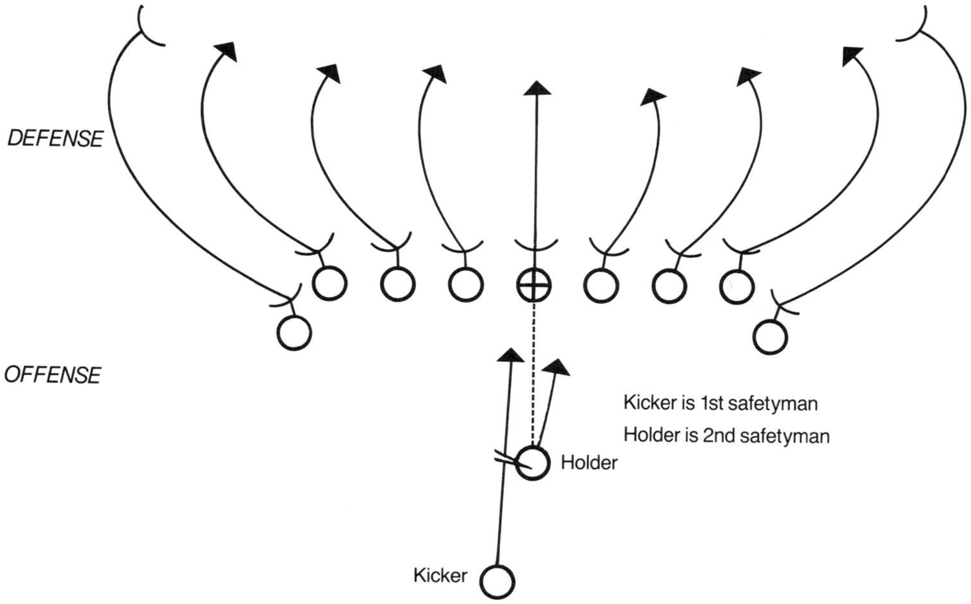

DEFENSE

OFFENSE

Kicker is 1st safetyman
Holder is 2nd safetyman

Holder

Kicker

their inside gaps. If no defensive man is entering their zones, they lean to the outside to cover as much lateral space as possible.

All of the men blocking to protect the kicker have the same assignment. *They must never let any rushing men penetrate to the inside.* If the field goal is missed, they cover the attempt.

When a field goal is missed, usually the kicker is blamed for the missed kick. Often it is not his fault. The accuracy of the snap from the center and the speed and accuracy with which the holder sets the ball on the tee—in profes-

Field-Goal Kicking

Gripping the Ball

The center grips the upper end of the ball in in his right hand and lays the palm and fingers of his left hand on the middle and slightly to the left side of the ball (A,B). This grip provides greater power and accuracy on the snap than the onehanded grip used in snaps to the quarterback.

A   B

sional football there is no tee and the ball must be kicked from the surface—must be perfectly timed. The holder takes his position. The center must snap the ball fast and accurately to the holder's hands. As the holder catches the ball and starts to place it on the tee, he should spin it so that the laces face the middle of the goalposts.

To time the kick properly, the kicker starts forward as he hears the ball hit the hands of the holder. There are two types of field-goal kickers, the soccer-style and the straight-ahead.

The Center's Snap to the Holder
The snap itself is quick and clean. The center should sight the holder before the snap and aim for the holder's outstretched hand (C,D).

C   D

Field-Goal Kicking: The Holder

A

B

Field-Goal Kicking: The Holder
Upon receipt of the ball from the center (A), the holder starts to position the ball so that the laces face toward the goalposts. He holds the ball by its end and sets it on

THE STRAIGHT-AHEAD FIELD-GOAL KICK

The straight-ahead is easier to execute than the soccer-style because the kicker only needs to swing his foot directly at the goalposts instead of coming from the side and then swinging the foot at the goalposts as the soccer-style kicker must do.

The kicker takes his position about two yards behind the kicking tee. As he hears the ball hit the holder's hands he takes a short step forward with his right foot (if he is a right-legged kicker), then a full stride with his left foot so that it hits the ground four to six inches behind and to the left of the kicking tee. Then, while keeping his eye on the ball, he tightens the ankle muscles of his kicking leg so that the ankle joint is stiff and virtually immobilized. His toe hits the ball slightly below the midpoint of the point and middle of the ball. He powerfully swings his foot through the ball on the line for the middle of the goalposts.

C   D

the tee (B). If the laces are still not facing toward the goalposts, he spins the ball with his right hand so that they are (C). Then he makes sure the ball is upright for the kicker (D). All of this requires speed and dexterity.

Kicking Tees

Soccer-style   **Straight-ahead**

The Straight-Ahead Field-Goal Kick

A

B

C

The right-footed kicker stands about two yards behind the tee. At the moment he hears the ball hit the holder's hands, he takes a short step with his right foot (A), followed by a full stride with his left foot (B), so that the left foot lands four to six inches behind and to the left of the kicking tee. Then with the ankle of his kicking leg locked, he kicks through the ball, slightly below its midline (C).

Mark Mosely of the Redskins is a classic straight-ahead field-goal kicker. He binds his right shoe so tightly that it immobilizes his ankle. He makes his kicks rise quickly to get the ball over the linemen, and he has good range.

The straight-ahead kicker has two recurring problems. He must be certain his left foot does not skid or slide as it hits the ground, and he must adjust the angle of his kick to compensate for any wind coming from either side.

THE SOCCER-STYLE FIELD-GOAL KICK

The soccer-style kicker usually has greater length because a larger portion of his foot hits the ball and the velocity of the kicking foot is slightly faster than with the straight-ahead kick. The soccer-style kicker takes his position slightly more than a yard behind the holder and, if he is a right-footed kicker, about a yard to the left.

When he hears the ball hit the holder's hands, he takes a short step with his right foot toward the holder. He then strides forward with his left foot and places it on the ground about six inches behind and to the left of the tee. He pivots slightly on this foot as he swings his right leg from the side through the ball on a line to the middle of the goalposts.

The kicker watches the ball as it is placed on the tee and hits it with his instep just below the midpoint of the point and middle of the ball. As in the straight-ahead kick, the soccer-style kicker must keep his eye on the point of the ball he wants to hit with his instep. He must never look up. He swings his leg from the hip and accelerates the kick by using his knee and calf muscles. He then follows through on the line to the middle of the goalposts while still watching the point where his foot has met the ball.

Obviously, the soccer-style kicker must be certain his left foot does not slip. If he loses this base, it will be impossible to turn his body, swing his leg and follow through accurately on the kick.

Young kickers, whether they use the straight-ahead or soccer-style kick, must practice their step-and-a-half approach to the ball until they can take the short step and stride accurately, positioning the left foot perfectly prior to executing the kick. They should develop a positive rhythm—hear the ball hit the holder's hands, step with the right foot, stride with the left foot, and then execute the kick. They should learn to develop that rhythmic technique without worrying about how far they will kick the ball. When they can mechanically, perfectly, accurately take the step and a half, they can work to develop more power from the kicking leg.

The Soccer-Style Field-Goal Kick

The right-footed kicker stands slightly deeper than a yard behind the holder and about a yard to the left, his left foot advanced toward the ball (A). When the ball hits the holder's hands, the kicker takes a step with his right foot and a stride with his left foot (B). Then he kicks, pivoting slightly on his left foot, hitting the ball with the instep of his right foot just below the middle of the ball. Note how straight he keeps his kicking leg on the approach and follow-through (C).

Whenever a field-goal attempt is tried further than 25 yards from the goal line, all men on the kicking team must assume the kick will be short and possible to return.

Covering a field-goal attempt

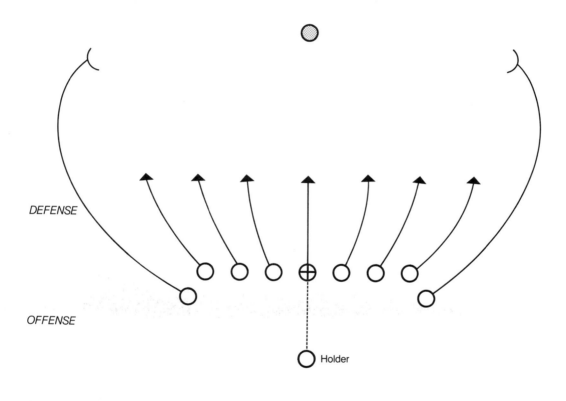

After executing their blocks as described above to protect the kicker, the two wingbacks move to their outside on a 45-degree angle and then turn downfield after they are wide enough to be certain the kick return man will be forced to run to their inside. The center goes straight downfield at the man who may receive the ball. The guards start downfield and move to the outside about four yards from the center. The tackles move downfield and widen so that they are four to five yards outside the guards. The ends start downfield and widen so that they are five yards outside their tackles. All men run downfield on these courses as fast as possible and close on the ballcarrier to make the tackle.

The kicker is the first safety man. If the kick is short and can be returned, he runs about half-speed downfield at the man who has caught the ball. The kicker positions himself directly in front of the man, where he can make the tackle if the ballcarrier gets past the other cover men. The holder is the true safety. After the ball is kicked, he moves laterally to either side to place himself in front of the man who has caught the ball, and he stays in position to make the tackle if the receiver gets to him.

FAKE KICK PLAYS

When the defensive team is intent on blocking the kick, it becomes vulnerable to fake kick plays. Two of the most common in all levels of football are *the pass-run option* and *the screen pass to the kicker*.

Pass-Run Option

In the option play, the center snaps the ball to the holder as he would normally and the blockers block exactly as they would if the kick were being made. The holder places the ball on the tee—but as he does, if it is a college or high school team, he must raise his knee off the ground or else he will be ineligible to run with the ball.

The kicker makes a perfect swing just as though he were kicking the ball, and as he follows through and moves in front of the holder, the holder picks the ball off the tee and begins to roll to the outside.

The rushing men usually try to get in front of the line of the kick. This makes it easy for the holder to get outside of all the rushing men. If the holder's tight end is open, he can throw the ball to him. If the defensive halfback drops back to cover the end, the holder can usually run for substantial yardage.

Fake field goal—pass-run option

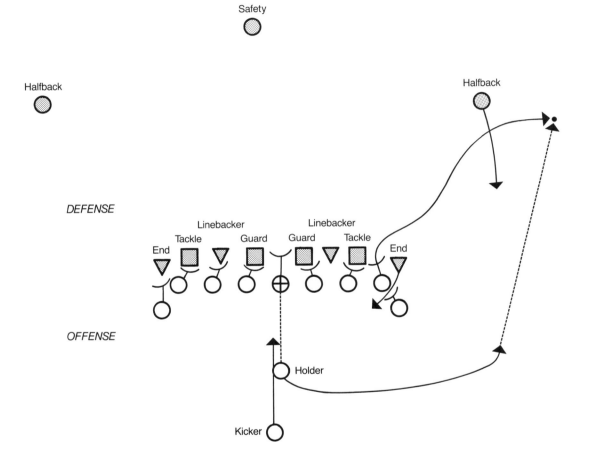

Safety

Halfback

Halfback

DEFENSE

Linebacker   Linebacker

Tackle   Guard   Guard   Tackle

End   End

OFFENSE

Holder

Kicker

Screen Pass to the Kicker

The beginning of the screen play is executed exactly as the pass-run option. The kicker, after faking the kick, turns and watches the holder as he runs to the outside. Then the kicker, acting unconcerned, drifts away from the holder and drops back slightly so that he will be behind the holder. The offensive linemen, after blocking their opponents in normal fashion, slide into position in front of the kicker. After rolling wide to the outside, the holder stops and throws the ball back to the kicker who uses his blockers to make a substantial gain on the play.

Fake field goal—screen pass to the kicker

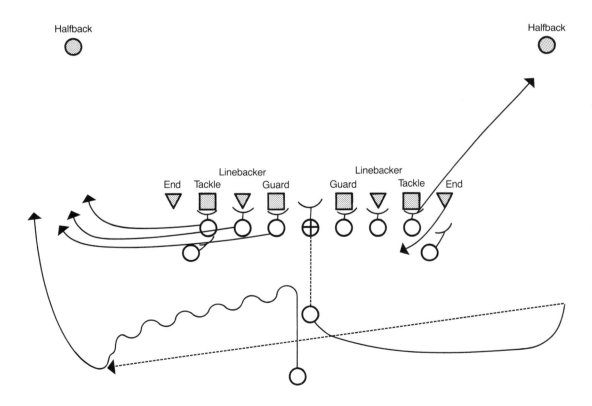

Usually this play is totally successful if the holder has time to move to the outside and throw the ball accurately back to the kicker. The defensive team has been expecting the field goal. When the ball is not kicked and the holder rolls to the outside, the entire defensive team reacts to this movement. They become so intent on stopping the holder from either running or throwing the ball downfield that they fail to recognize that the kicker is an eligible pass receiver and rarely place themselves in position to cover him properly. It is easy for him to drift outside of the entire defensive team, catch the ball, and make a long gain. The play should be a lateral pass because if the receiver goes downfield for a forward pass, he is much more likely to be covered.

Building the Offensive Game Plan

A coach must take two basic factors into account when designing his team's offensive game plan—the defense used by the opponents and the strength of the offensive team.

ANALYZING THE OPPONENT'S DEFENSE

Most defensive teams play one basic alignment. From this set, they usually adjust it slightly to complicate the blocking assignments of the offensive team. In setting up the offensive game plan, the coach should first analyze the basic alignment used by the opponent, together with the variations that it employs.

Next, he should analyze the pass defense. Most teams favor either the "man-for-man" or the "zone." Since different pass plays are better against the zone and others against the man-for-man, *the pass offense should be designed to take advantage of the pass defense generally used by the opponent.*

For example, if the opponents' basic pass defense is a zone and their alignment has four line-

167

An effective offensive game plan requires clear communication between coach and players.

men, three linebackers, two cornerbacks, a strong safety, and a weak safety, the cornerman to the side of the split end will cover his deep third of the field. The weak safety covers the deep middle third of the field, and the strong safety covers the deep third to the side of the tight end. The cornerback to the side of the tight end covers the flat zone to his side. The linebacker to the side of the split end covers the outside flat zone to his side, and the linebacker over the tight end and the middle linebacker cover the two inside short zones.

On the play, there are more receivers than defenders to cover all the zones. The two wide receivers move downfield rapidly and then run a hook pattern at a depth of eight yards. The tight end goes downfield slightly to his outside and then at six yards' depth, hooks to his inside. The left halfback moves downfield slightly to his outside and hooks at a depth of six yards. The passer watches the middle linebacker and throws to either his tight end or left halfback —whichever man is not covered by the middle linebacker.

Pass play against the 4-3-4 Zone Pass Defense
The passer throws to the left halfback or tight end—the man not covered by the middle linebacker.

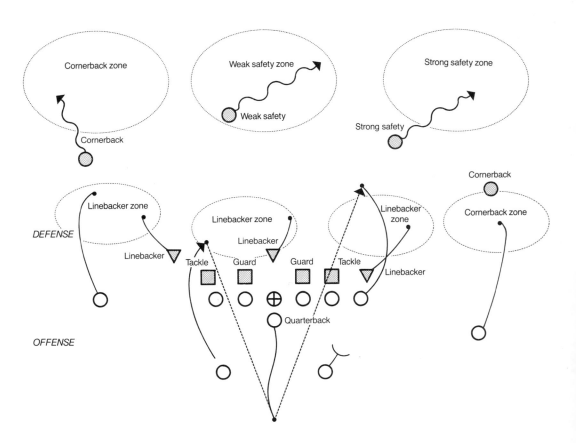

When the defensive team uses a man-for-man pass defense, the two corner-backs cover the outside receivers. The strong safety covers the tight end, and the weak safety drops back and covers the field as a "free man" to assist in making the tackle if a receiver catches the ball. The linebackers to the left and right side cover the halfback who comes to their side. The middle linebacker is free to concentrate on watching the quarterback and moving to the ball after it is thrown.

Against this man-for-man defense, any receiver can get open by running a good pass route against the defensive man assigned to cover him. For exam-ple, the split end is supposed to be covered by a cornerback. He starts downfield aiming for a spot three yards outside the defender. At a depth of 10 yards, he curls to the inside and sets up as though the quarterback were going to throw the ball to him on a hook pattern. As the quarterback fakes the throw of the hook pattern, the split end quickly breaks to his outside. Usually, the corner-

Pass play against Man-for-Man Pass Defense
The quarterback fakes a pass to the split end as he runs a curl pattern, then passes when the split end breaks to the outside.

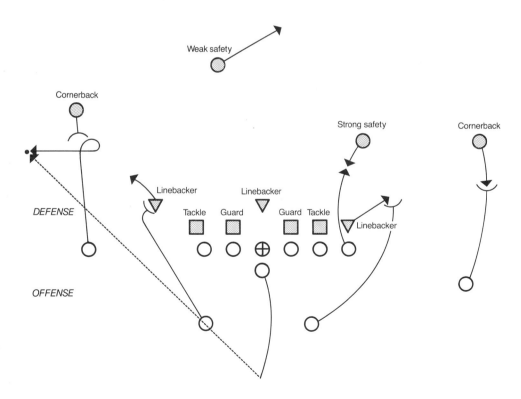

back will have started up and in to cover the "curl pattern." When the receiver breaks to the outside, the defender moving up and in will be unable to adjust his course to cover the split end who will now be open to catch the pass.

Most defensive teams have "tendencies" on different down-and-yardage situations. When it is long yardage, for example, the linebackers will usually play deeper and the secondary men will be more conscious of the pass than of the run. In that situation, inside running plays are usually very effective—particularly if the movement of the quarterback fakes a pass play.

The center blocks the guard to his left. The left guard executes the trap block on the defensive left guard. The right guard drops back faking a pass-protection block and takes any man coming into his zone as does the right tackle. The tight end starts downfield about four yards and then breaks to his

Inside run on long yardage

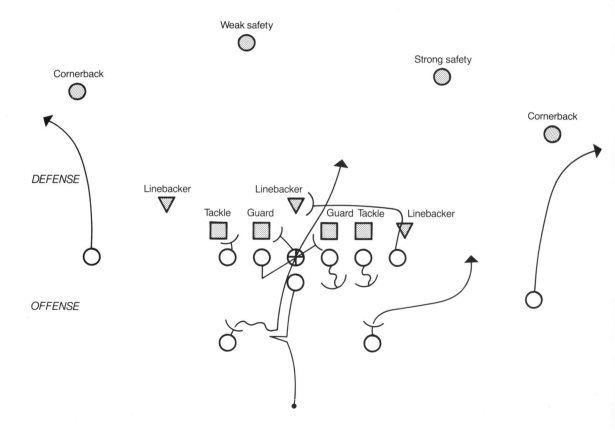

inside and uses a shoulder block to knock the middle linebacker to the left. The left tackle blocks the man over him. Each wide receiver goes downfield 10 yards and breaks to his outside. Each halfback fakes a pass-protection block. Then, the right halfback curls to his outside. The left halfback moves to his inside and takes the ball from the quarterback, who fakes dropping back to throw. The ballcarrier then breaks inside between the blocks of the center and the trapping guard and outside the middle linebacker.

In short yardage situations, the defensive team usually plays closer to the line of scrimmage and strives for penetration to prevent any offensive gain. This makes it relatively easy to run effectively to the outside. The center blocks the guard to his left. The right guard, tackle, and tight end all block their opponents to the inside. The left guard leads around and turns upfield just outside of the

Outside run on short yardage

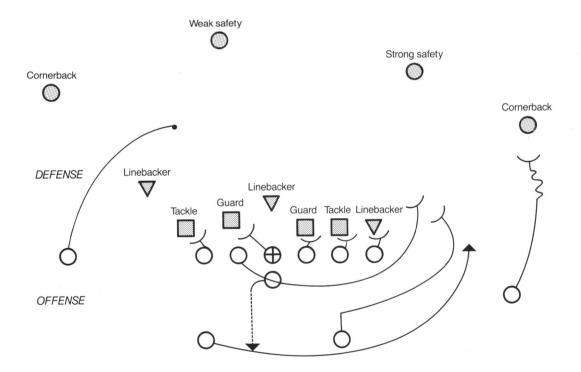

block of the tight end. The left tackle blocks the opponent over him. The flankerback starts downfield and then "stalks" the defensive cornerback blocking him while reacting to stop the run. The split end moves to his inside, fakes a hook pattern, and watches the play. The right halfback takes a step forward and then moves to his outside and turns upfield just outside the pulling left guard. He blocks the first opponent to come into his path. The quarterback turns and tosses the ball back to the left halfback, who runs the sweep play to his right. When the defense is striving for penetration, the blocks described are not difficult and the play is usually successful.

The defensive team is always acutely aware of the down-and-yardage situation.

On normal down-and-yardage situations, the defenders do not expect any particular play and gear up to stop any play that may be run. The offensive team should then use its regular plays, which if properly executed will gain an average of four or five yards.

In long yardage situations—when the offensive team must average more than five yards per play to make a first down—the defenders are usually pass-conscious. Before the snap, they are mentally prepared to rush the passer and cover the receivers. That makes them vulnerable to fake-pass running plays hitting inside.

On short yardage situations—when the offensive team needs to make only two yards or less for a first down—the defense is mentally prepared to get penetration along the line of scrimmage to stop the play for no gain at all. That makes them vulnerable to sweep plays to the outside.

In designing their offensive game plan, coaches should include plays that will be effective against the defensive tendencies and mental patterns of the defensive team on normal, long, and short yardage situations.

ANALYZING YOUR TEAM'S CAPACITIES

Different men on your team have different degrees of ability. Carefully evaluate each man against the opponent he will face. Decide, for example, which lineman is most likely to be able to beat his opponent the majority of the time. Having done that, use the plays that take advantage of your man's superior ability as the basic part of your offensive plan.

The fundamental decision that must be made in building the game plan is whether your team has enough physical strength to control the line of scrimmage and keep possession of the ball. When the coach believes this can be done, most of the plays used should be designed for consistent short gains.

If you do not believe your team has the physical ability to dominate the defensive team with a ball-control game, the offensive game plan should be designed to set up potential long-gain, breakaway plays such as reverses, reverse passes, and other "trick plays."

POINTS TO REMEMBER WHEN BUILDING THE OFFENSIVE GAME PLAN

Before the advent of television, scouting was an inexact science. Today, TV covers many high school and college games. In addition, all teams film their games. Many schools and conferences have well-defined rules for the exchange of films. When such arrangements are not made, it is still reasonably easy for a coach to get a tape or film record of each coming opponent through his local TV station.

That gives coaches the opportunity to analyze carefully the play of each coming opponent. Thus, there can be no surprises about what a team has done in the past or the skills possessed by its individual players. The only possible surprise is the use of formations and plays that have not been shown in previous games. The further the season progresses, the more unlikely that becomes since there is a limit to the number of formations and plays an offensive team can run. Teams usually win or lose depending on their ability to execute well their fundamental offensive patterns.

At the college level and in professional football, computers are used to analyze quickly the field position and down-and-distance tendencies of the opponent to be played. That is done by recording the plays run from each section of the field. Also included in the record is the lateral field position of the ball and whether the play was run on normal, long, or short yardage.

When all of this information is put into the computer, the machine prints out the total defensive tendencies of the opponent. That is a valuable aide to the coach in planning his offensive game plan.

It must be noted, however, that the opponent is using the same techniques. He is using his computer records to analyze the tendencies of your team. He knows as much about your team as you do about his.

In addition, almost all coaches use those techniques to analyze their own team so that they have in hand, while making their game plan, the same information their opponents possess regarding the tendencies the team has shown in previous games.

By using that information properly, a coaching staff can develop a game

Head coach Bill Walsh of the San Francisco Forty-Niners is renowned for his meticulously prepared game plans.

plan that will surprise the opponent because in every situation it uses plays different from those that were previously run. For example, if your team, in previous games, has had a strong tendency to run inside plays on short yardage, the game plan should be altered so that wide plays will be called on short yardage situations. Likewise, if your team has rarely thrown a pass on first down, the game plan should be designed to throw on first down perhaps 60 percent of the time. By making those adjustments, the offensive team will be running the least expected plays in all situations.

A difficult decision the coach must make in deciding his game plan is the number of plays that will be included in his offense for each game: how many passes, how many runs.

In a normal game, the offensive team will have the ball for only 50 to 55 snaps. Plays must be included in the offensive "ready" list for long yardage, short yardage, and normal yardage. All plays must be practiced enough times to ensure proper execution during the game.

Most offensive teams use signal systems that give them an almost unlimited number of play choices. Such systems will enable the team to use almost any formation, run every conceivable pass pattern, include straight-ahead running plays, traps, reverses. The problem the coach faces in preparing for each game is the selection of those plays from the signal system that have the best chance of success against the opponent to be played.

If the offense can expect to have the ball for only 50 to 55 snaps, it is foolish to have more than 45 plays on the ready list: The other five or ten snaps will be almost predetermined: punts, field goals, and short yardage plays.

Assuming the team is equally effective throwing the ball and running it, the ready list should have about half passes and half runs—22 or 23 passes, and 22 or 23 runs. If the team is more effective throwing the ball than running it, the number of passes on the ready list should be a higher percentage than the runs. In that case, the offensive plan should include 30 to 32 passes, which would reduce the number of running plays to 13 or 15. Conversely, if your team executes the running attack better than the pass attack, you would include 30 to 32 runs and only 13 to 15 passes on the ready list.

When the "ready" list has more than 45 plays, the game will usually be over before all the plays can be used. The time spent in practice on the unused plays is time wasted.

To repeat, offensive football is a game of meticulous execution. Diligent competitive practices are required to learn to run each play well. Limiting the number of plays to be used in any game—the "ready" list for the particular contest—will enable the offensive team to have adequate practice time to learn to execute those plays flawlessly.

Practice Schedules

Conference and national rules limit the amount of practice time available to high school and college teams. Professionals obviously have unlimited practice time.

At any level of football—cub, high school, college, or professional—each player, during the off-season, should work out on a regular schedule and develop his body so that he will be in the best possible overall physical condition when the practice sessions begin.

Football is a game of movement. The ability to run is the most important physical attribute required. In preparing for the beginning of practice sessions, each player, as a part of each workout, should do some distance running, usually a half-mile to a mile a day, and combine this distance running with a series of sprints—ten 10-yard sprints, ten 20-yard sprints, and six 40-yard sprints. (Forty yards is usually the maximum distance run by any player on any play in a game.)

In addition to running, each player should develop his muscle structure. If Nautilus machines are available, they should be used. If Nautilus equipment is not available, players should lift weights at their school, local YMCA, or boys' club.

177

In-season practice should emphasize team execution more than fundamentals.

A combination of running drills and bodybuilding exercises makes it possible for each man to develop his maximum overall physical condition before the beginning of practice. The level of condition achieved by an athlete before practices start is an accurate barometer for the coach regarding the player's dedication to the game. Players who report for practice overweight and in poor condition obviously have lacked the self-discipline to achieve prime condition. In all probability, these men will not practice with any more dedication. Men who are in prime condition demonstrate to the coach on the opening day of practice that they are dedicated to the game and desire to make the maximum contribution to the team's success.

School and conference rules limit the number of off-season meetings that a coach can have with his team. In all instances, however, at least two meetings are allowed. At those sessions, the coach should explain the off-season conditioning program described above so that each man understands what he needs to do to develop his body to be ready for practice. Also, at those sessions the coach should explain the importance of diligent off-season practice. Any team that begins practice in poor condition will be subject to injuries and will lack the stamina to perform well during practice. If they attempt to "practice themselves into condition," they will have lost valuable time in fundamental preparation.

Practices are designed to teach players to play the game—not to condition them. Any conditioning that does occur is a by-product.

Football practices fall into three basic categories: spring practice, early fall practice, and individual game preparation.

PLANS AND OBJECTIVES FOR SPRING PRACTICE

For coaches, spring practice has two basic objectives: first, to teach each player to execute the fundamentals of the game, and second, to evaluate the players available for the coming season and place them in the position they will play to contribute most to the success of the team.

Before the start of each practice, the team should meet in a classroom, lecture situation. At that time, the coaches should explain each drill that will be done during practice that day and diagram each play that will be taught. The team then goes to the practice field to execute the schedule that has been explained through the lecture.

During spring practice, the team needs to learn only enough plays to have an adequate offense for scrimmages: about ten runs and eight passes. The running plays should hit each spot along the line of scrimmage. The pass plays should be designed to throw at least once to each eligible receiver.

Time should never be spent in teaching a great number of runs, passes, or formation variations. Practice time should be devoted to developing the individual skills of the players and making certain that each man is placed in the position where he will be most productive.

OBJECTIVES OF EARLY FALL PRACTICE

During the summer, the coaching staff should write a letter each week to each player on the team. Those letters explain in detail what each man needs to do to condition himself properly for the coming season. They also explain the basic signal system, formations, and plays that will constitute the basic offense. Each letter should contain a short inspirational message realistically explaining the attitude each player must develop—unselfish in all respects—if he hopes to make the greatest possible contribution to the team.

The coach, through this constant communication with his players during the summer, begins to establish the relationship that must exist during the season—total confidence in each other and dedication to a victorious season—between the players and the coaching staff. By doing this before early fall practice, he gives the players a clear understanding of what is expected of them.

During the first week of early fall practice, the coaching staff should carefully re-evaluate the decisions made in spring practice regarding the position each player will play during the season. If position changes are to be made, they should be made during the first week.

The next objectives of early fall practice are to improve each player's execution of the fundamental skills he needs and to teach the team the basic offensive plays and signal system that will be used during the season.

As was done in spring practice, the coaches should meet with the players in a lecture-type meeting before each practice. The lecture will explain in detail exactly which drills will be done at what time and which plays will be taught at the practice session. Then the actual practice can be devoted to developing needed skills without taking time on the field to explain how the drills are to be done and what the players' assignments are on each play to be practiced.

Different coaches have their own methods of teaching plays. Some have them mimeographed and give the play sheets to the players. I believe it is far better to have each player diagram each play as the coach explains it on the blackboard. That ensures that each man is actively involved.

Each day the plays discussed and explained are added to a loose-leaf notebook, which becomes the player's playbook for the season.

At each practice, players in each position should work on their fundamentals—starts, blocks, hand-offs, pass patterns, etc. After the individual drills have been completed, the team is brought together to be taught running and passing plays. The first plays taught should be those that were used in spring practice, providing something of a review for the players. After all plays used in spring practice have been reviewed and reinstalled as in the offensive system, new formations and plays are introduced. Three running plays and three new passes should be installed at each practice session until the entire basic offense has been taught to the team. As the new plays are being taught, plays the team already knows are constantly reviewed.

When the team is one week away from its first game, the practice sessions are planned to prepare for the first opponent. At the team meeting on the first day of practice in preparation for the particular opponent, the coach gives a complete scouting report. That will include an explanation of the opponent's formations and plays as well as an analysis of its "tendencies." Also, the strength and probable weaknesses of each individual player to be faced are honestly discussed and evaluated.

The coach then explains his game plan for the coming contest. He lists all the plays that will be on the "ready" list. While doing so, he "sells" the team on why the plan will be effective. The players must truly believe the plan is excellent and, if executed properly, will enable them to win. This gives them the confidence they need to execute the plays flawlessly.

After the scouting reports and game plans have been thoroughly explained, the coach describes the practice schedule for the day so that each man knows exactly what he must do each minute during the practice.

It is important for the coach to recognize that the further his team progresses through the schedule, the less time needs to be spent in practice. The practice schedule trend should move away from emphasis on fundamentals toward emphasis on team execution. A player who has been through spring and early fall practice and has played four or five games is already about as capable in his fundamentals as he will be this season. It is far better to concentrate on each player's timing and execution on team plays and to shorten practice by not spending so much time on fundamentals. That makes it possible for the players to be fresh and rested for the coming game.

Different coaches have different theories about the duration of practice during the season. As a rule, I believe, most coaches are inclined to overwork their teams. A player who is physically and mentally tired is unable to perform to his potential. If he is rested, he can play up to his ability.

We had an understanding on our coaching staff at Oklahoma that after we had planned our practice schedule, if any coach on the staff thought we were going to be on the field too long, the schedule was changed and shortened to the time that coach felt we could work and still be fresh for the coming game. I know this coaching philosophy paid big dividends. Our team was almost always better rested than our opponent. This enabled our men to perform at their maximum ability in each game and was a basic reason why our club was able to win most of the time.

MID-SEASON DAILY PRACTICE SCHEDULE

MONDAY: Players who participated in the game the previous Saturday work out on their own in sweat suits for approximately 20 minutes. After their warmup, the team is brought together and taught the new plays that will be used against the opponent in the coming game. This session should last only 10 to 15 minutes.

The men who did not play in the game the previous week scrimmage against their counterparts on the defensive team for 30 to 40 minutes. The scrimmage serves to keep all squad players competitive and in a "contact" mood.

TUESDAY: Kickers, pass receivers, throwers, and other specialty men should be on the field 20 minutes before formal practice begins, to loosen their muscles and practice their specialties. The schedule below assumes men are out of classes and are available to practice by 3 p.m.

3:30	Warmup stretching and bending exercises.
3:35	Three segments of the team—offensive linemen, backs, and wide receivers—work in groups practicing their individual fundamentals. Tight ends spend half their time with the offensive line and the other half working with the wide receivers.
3:55	Offensive linemen continue group work. Backs and all receivers join to practice pass offense.
4:25	The team comes together and practices the offensive plays to be used in the game against a defensive team that uses the defensive alignments of the opponent.

4:55	Practice punt protection and coverage.
5:10	Practice field goals and extra points.
5:25	Run sprints. The entire squad lines up on a single yard line. The quarterback uses his regular starting count as the signal to start each sprint. The first four sprints are five yards in length. The players have 10 yards in which to slow down, stop, and turn around to sprint in the opposite direction. After the four five-yard sprints, four 10-yard sprints are run in exactly the manner as described above. The squad then runs two 20-yard sprints in the same manner, and finishes with two 40-yard sprints.
5:35	Practice over.

WEDNESDAY:

3:30	Warmup stretching and bending exercises.
3:35	Offensive linemen and wide receivers work in groups practicing their fundamentals.
3:50	Offensive linemen continue group work. Backs and receivers join to practice pass offense.
4:15	The team joins together and runs against a defensive team that uses the defenses expected to be played by the opponent.
4:40	Practice punt protection and coverage.
5:00	Practice field goals and extra points.
5:10	Run sprints, as described above, but fewer: The session consists of two 5-yard sprints, two 10-yard sprints, one 20-yard sprint, and one 40-yard sprint.
5:15	Practice over.

THURSDAY:

3:30	Warmup stretching and bending exercises.
3:35	Offensive linemen, backs, and wide receivers do group work. Line continues group work. Backs and receivers practice offense.
4:05	Team work.
4:25	Practice punt protection and coverage.
4:35	Practice field goals and PATs.
4:45	Practice over.

3:30	Warmup stretching.
3:35	Review all offensive plays on the "ready" list.
4:05	Review punting game.
4:10	Review place kick game.
4:15	Review kickoff returns.
4:20	Practice over.

MENTAL PREPARATION

The mental attitude of the squad before any game is the cumulative result of the training the men have received in the preseason meetings, spring practice, and early fall practice. During these sessions, each player must be taught to make his total, all-out effort on every drill and every play run during each practice.

The coaching staff constantly monitors this effort level, and when a player does not make his best effort, he should be quietly criticized and reminded that unless he can learn to play consistently to the best of his ability he will never develop to his true potential. Players should be corrected but not criticized in front of their teammates during practice sessions.

If any player, with or without much potential, consistently fails to try his best in practice sessions, the coach should ask the man to visit his office. At this personal meeting, the coach should explain to the player his shortcomings without embarrassing him in front of his teammates. If the player does not improve his level of effort in the next few practices, he should be dropped from the team. The old axiom that "one rotten apple destroys the barrel" applies here. If any man is allowed to loaf his way through practice sessions, it has a debilitating effect on the rest of the squad. If any man is allowed to continue practice while not making his best effort, his example will soon have other members of the team making less than their best effort. This is always a disaster. The team that does not practice well can never play well.

All football players must be taught to understand and believe that they are not actually competing in football to defeat an opponent. Rather, the game only gives them the opportunity to compete against and to test themselves.

In some games a player will face an opponent who is inferior in his physical ability. It will be easy to defeat him. In other games, he will face a man of superior ability. Rarely will he be able to defeat him. In either case, the true

Team preparation and solid coaching are at the heart of successful football. Equally important is a positive rapport between team and coach.

objective and the test for each player is simply, "Did I make my best effort on every play?"

It is always essential throughout the season that coaches and players are totally honest with each other. The best way of teaching each man always to make his best effort is through "heart-to-heart" honest acknowledgments by the players of their effort in practice.

For example, after the third or fourth practice, the coach assembles the team in the locker room immediately after the session has ended. He asks the question, "How many of you did your all-out best today on each drill and every play? If you did, raise your hand." If the players are honest, no one will raise his hand, because it takes time to learn always to make the best effort. The coach then repeats his explanation as to why such an effort is needed if they expect to win.

Two or three days later, after practice, he again gathers the squad together and asks the same question. This time, probably four or five men will raise their hands because they have learned to test and discipline themselves never to coast on any drill or play.

The sequence is repeated every three or four days until everyone on the squad, in all honesty, is able to raise his hand when asked, "Did you do your best on every drill and every play?"

When this level of effort is achieved, the team will play as well as it can against every opponent.

The thought that a coach can deliver an inspirational pregame or halftime speech to change drastically and improve his team's performance is a myth. Teams play only as well as they have learned to do in practice. When the players have learned always to make their best effort on every play, they will perform up to their potential.

13

How to Watch Offensive Football

All football games are exciting spectacles. The bands, cheerleaders, and expectant crowd combine to create an air of high excitement. During the pregame warmup drills, the skills of the specialists—kickers, passers, and receivers—are displayed. The size and quickness of the linebackers and linemen gives a foretaste of the excitement to come.

It is possible to enjoy a football game without knowing much about the strategies involved. The electric excitement and the crowd's reaction to outstanding plays bring elation to people in the stands—even though they may not know much about the techniques or rules of the game.

The most common mistake spectators make is to concentrate almost exclusively on the ball. By using peripheral vision and learning to scan the entire field before and after the ball is snapped, spectators can see much more of the game and enjoy it more.

When the offensive team breaks the huddle and lines up, the spectator should be able to recognize immediately the formation being used. Then the spectator should look at the defense and the pattern it is playing. How many men are on the line of scrimmage? How many linebackers are

187

To enjoy a football game more, spectators should learn to scan the entire field before and after the snap.

there, and how deep are they playing? Is the defense using two cornerbacks and two safeties, or a three-deep defense with a "rover" or "monster" back? If a player goes in motion before the snap, the spectator should recognize the defensive adjustment made to cover the change in offensive formation.

Watching Offensive Football:
What to Look for Before the Snap

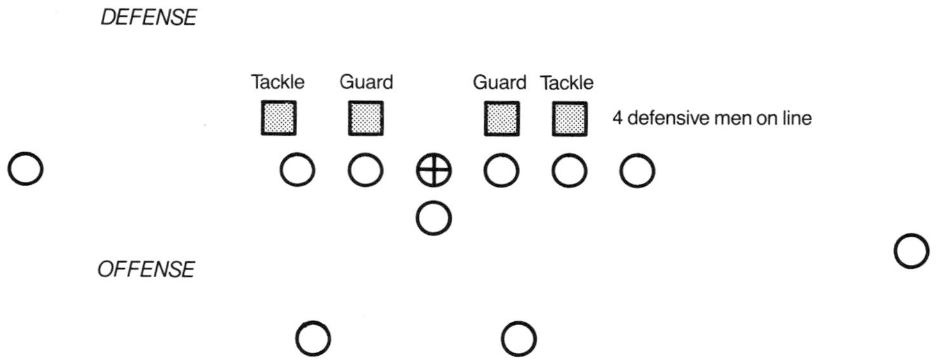

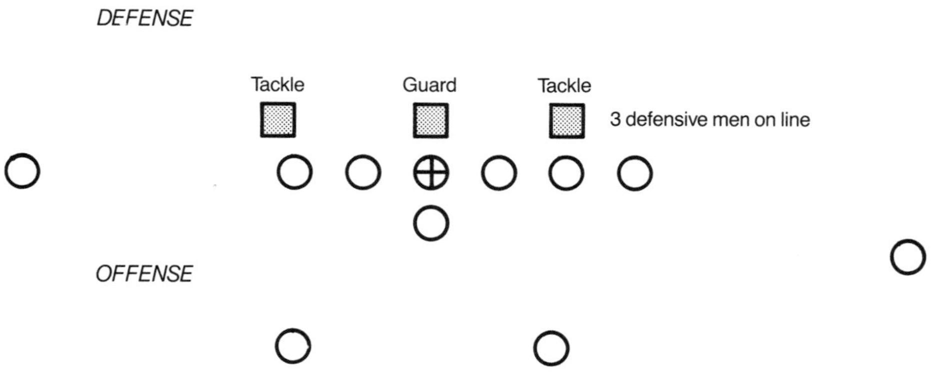

DEFENSE

Tackle Guard Guard Tackle

4 defensive men on line

OFFENSE

DEFENSE

Tackle Guard Tackle

3 defensive men on line

OFFENSE

A

- How many defensive men are on the line of scrimmage?
- How many linebackers are playing and how deep are they lined up?
- Is the defense using two cornermen and two safeties?
- Or is the defense playing a three-deep defense with a "rover" or "monster" back?

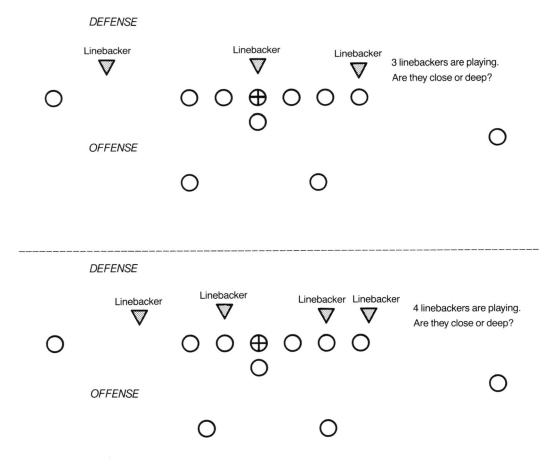

Watching Offensive Football:
What to Look for Before the Snap (Cont.)

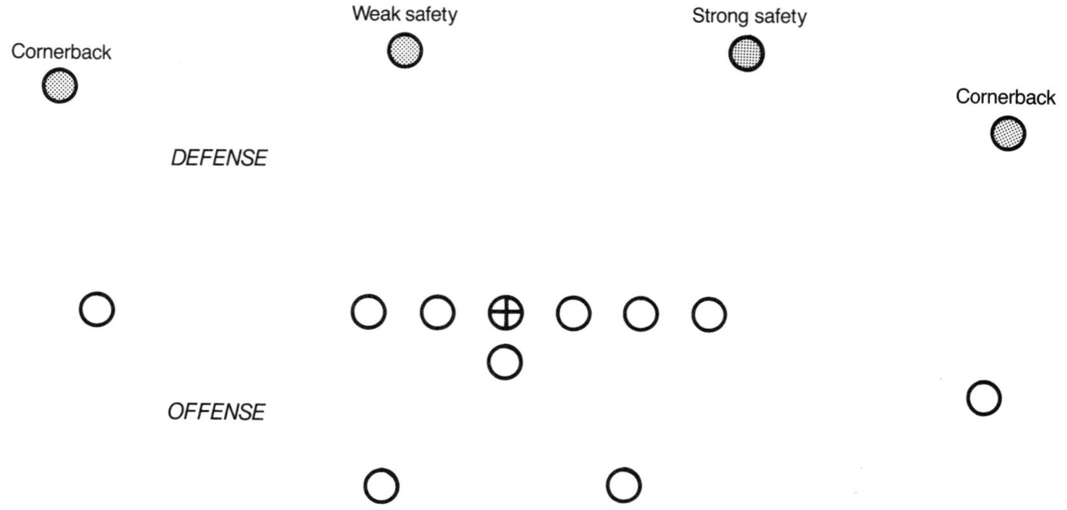

Weak safety

Strong safety

Cornerback

Cornerback

DEFENSE

OFFENSE

C: Two cornermen, two safeties.

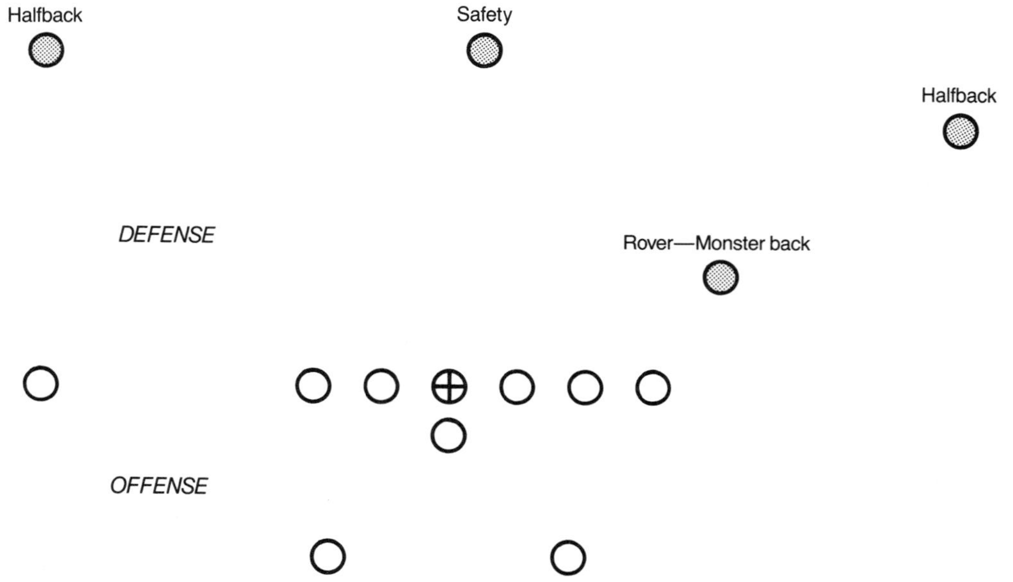

Halfback

Safety

Halfback

DEFENSE

Rover—Monster back

OFFENSE

D: Three-deep defense with "rover" or "monster" back.

Some people enjoy the game more by trying to anticipate the offensive play to be run. If they have guessed correctly and the play makes yardage, they realize they are great field generals. If an unexpected play has been called and it fails, the would-be quarterbacks have the satisfaction of believing that if their play had been called, a gain would have been made. In that regard, all coaches realize that the only truly successful play is one that makes yardage. Whether the play anticipated by the spectator is actually used or not, if the play run gains yardage, everyone is happy.

To enjoy the game to the fullest, spectators must train themselves to see most of the field and to concentrate, before the snap of the ball, on *not looking at the ball.* When the play begins, the movements of the offensive and defensive players inevitably close in on the ball. The spectator will be able to locate it easily by watching the interplay of offensive and defensive men.

WHAT TO LOOK FOR AS THE BALL IS SNAPPED

At the snap, concentrate first on the offensive linemen. Their first move will indicate pass or run. If they charge forward across the line of scrimmage, the play will be a run. If they step back to protect the passer, the play will be a pass—unless it is a draw play or a screen pass.

Watching Offensive Football:
What to Look for as the Ball is Snapped

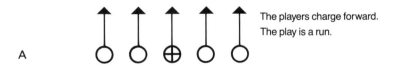

The players charge forward.
The play is a run.

A

The players step back. The play is a pass (or draw or screen).

B

Next, watch the pattern of the offensive team. If the play is a run, the blockers will lead to the man with the ball. If the play is a pass, immediately look at the defensive secondary to see the adjustments that are made as the receivers move downfield. It will be immediately apparent whether the defense is playing a man-for-man or zone defense. In turn, that will communicate to the spectator which defensive man was beaten or defended adequately on a man-for-man defense, or which defender did or did not cover his zone.

It requires practice and discipline for the spectator to learn to watch the game as described above. To repeat, in sequence:

1. Ascertain the offensive formation.
2. Recognize the defensive alignment being used.
3. When the ball is snapped, *do not watch the ball.* Instead, watch the pattern of play being run and the reactions of the defense.

By learning to recognize the offensive formation and the defense being used *before the ball is snapped,* the spectator will know the basic strategy of both teams. *By not watching the ball* when it is snapped—but instead watching the pattern of the offensive play and the defensive team's reactions, the spectator will see and know why the play was successful or why it failed. That should greatly increase understanding and enjoyment of the game.

HOW TO WATCH FOOTBALL ON TELEVISION

For many years I have had the good fortune to serve as a commentator on television broadcasts of football games. I am the "color" man working with the play-by-play announcer. To prepare for a game, I talk with both coaches. By understanding the two game plans, I am in position to evaluate which plan is proving to be most successful and, as the game progresses, to know which coaching staff is making the best adjustments.

It is always my desire and hope to explain to the audience why certain plays worked or failed. If I can do that, viewers will have an increased understanding of the tactics and strategies of the game. They also can recognize, particularly on replays, the strengths and weaknesses of the individual players.

The television cameras almost never show the entire offensive and defensive teams. Usually, the camera shows only the offensive linemen and backfield and the defensive linemen. Occasionally, the camera angle will be wide enough for the viewers to see the linebackers, too. At the start of any play, viewers rarely see the wide receivers or the defensive secondary.

Watching Offensive Football on Television

Before the ball is snapped:

- What is the offensive backfield set?

- How many defensive men are on the line of scrimmage?

- Can you see the linebackers? How deep are they playing?

When the ball is snapped:

- Are the offensive linemen charging across the line of scrimmage, or are they making pass-protection blocks?

- What is the pattern of blocking of the offensive team?

- By making these observations, you will pick up the ballcarrier on a run, or the quarterback and then the man to whom the ball is thrown on a pass play.

In my opinion, viewers would enjoy the game much more if directors used 195 a much wider-angled lens so that the viewer could see the entire offensive team and most of the defensive secondary. That would require an adjustment in TV production and viewing habits, but over a period of time it would lead to far greater enjoyment and understanding for viewers.

As in the stadium, the viewer should NOT WATCH THE BALL as the play begins. Instead, before the ball is snapped, he should, in sequence, learn to make the following observations:

1. Recognize the offensive backfield set.
2. Count the number of defensive men playing on the line of scrimmage.
3. If he can see any linebackers, note how deep they are playing.

When the ball is snapped, the viewer should:

1. Watch the offensive linemen—do they charge forward across the line of scrimmage, or do they make pass protection blocks?
2. Watch the pattern of the offensive blocking. That will eventually lead the viewer to the ballcarrier on a run or to the quarterback and then the receiver on pass plays.

It is quite simple, through disciplined habits of observation, to learn to watch each play in the sequence described. By so doing, the viewer will learn *not* to watch only the ball. Instead, before the ball is snapped, he will know the offensive formation and most of the basic defensive alignment. When the ball is snapped, he will quickly recognize whether the play is a pass or a run. And by following the pattern of play, he will recognize why it succeeded or failed.

Watching a televised football game this way will increase the viewer's enjoyment because he—or she—will understand the basic strategies being used and the reason the play succeeded or failed.

A Few Closing Remarks

As has been noted, football offense is a total team game. Each player must execute his assignment to perfection if the play is to succeed. It follows that through the experience of playing the game young men learn to understand and value the interdependence they share with their teammates.

No one player can "do it alone." A punter is dependent on the protection of his blockers. No matter how well he can punt the ball, if the blockers do not give him enough time, his skill is wasted. The same situation exists for placekickers, running backs, passers, and receivers. The man with the ball cannot overcome, through his own brilliance, inadequate play by his teammates.

One of the remarkable elements of football is the fact that the physical requirements for the various positions enable boys with widely differing sizes and abilities to make solid contributions to the team. Those who are big usually lack a degree of foot speed. Through diligent practice, however, they can become great offensive linemen. Men who are big—but lack the speed to be wide receivers can play effectively as tight ends. Smaller men who have good speed can learn to run pass patterns and catch the ball to become effective wide receivers. Backfield men who lack the elusiveness

197

and speed to be fine running backs, through diligent practice, can become outstanding blockers who clear the way for the ballcarriers. Men who lack the all-around athletic ability necessary to play any of those positions can become good punters or placekickers.

The widely varied skills required by the different positions make it possible for just about every boy who desires to be a football player to become an asset to his team.

I have one continuing argument with other members of the media. It has become commonplace to talk about the "skill" positions. When most commentators use this term, they are referring to the passers, receivers, and running backs. In my view, the term is totally misleading.

I believe the true "skill" positions are those of the offensive linemen and blocking backs. To make any play a success, each of these men must effectively block a tough, well-trained athlete. It takes far more skill to do this, play after play, than it does to run with the football or catch it.

I do accept the fact that the play of the quarterback requires great "skill." He is the heart and soul of the offensive team. His leadership and the confidence he displays give his teammates the conviction that by playing together they can move the ball. The T-formation quarterback begins each play, and his skilled execution is necessary for the success of every play. On running plays, he must hand or toss the ball correctly to his ballcarrier. He must be able to fake well on counter plays and reverses so that the defensive team will believe the man he fakes to actually has the ball. He must also be able to throw all types of passes —line-drive throws to short receivers; slightly arched tosses that go over the linebackers and are caught in front of the secondary; and long balls arched downfield to a receiver who is behind the entire secondary. To throw all of these types of passes, in varying wind and weather conditions, requires true skill.

My career as an active coach encompassed the changes from what some people call "old-fashioned football" to the modern game. During my first years as a coach, our team played the Single Wing. This formation was based on a powerful running game. Passes were always part of the attack, but usually the effectiveness of the running game spelled victory or defeat. The ability to block the opponent properly was fundamental to success.

In my first years at Oklahoma, our team played the Split-T formation. That offense did not require the same effective blocking needed in the Single Wing. Our offensive linemen—the guards, tackles, and ends—split one to two yards away from the center and each other. That spread the defense and created large gaps between the defenders before the snap of the ball. The offensive linemen blocked their opponent by charging at him and attempting to take him

Normal Offensive Line Spacing vs. Split-T Spacing

Normal

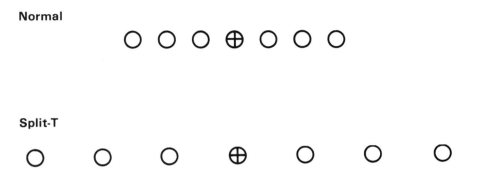

Split-T

to the proper side. If the defender fought through "the pressure" and was successful, the blocker simply maintained contact. Now, the ballcarrier, by watching the defensive man, could "run for daylight" by breaking to the opposite side.

That was a drastic change in offensive theory. No matter how effectively the defensive man avoided the opponent who was trying to block him, he still found it difficult to tackle the ballcarrier. This was a true breakthrough in theory when analyzed against the Single Wing formation. In the Single Wing, the play was successful only if the blockers were able to handle their opponents. In the Split-T, with the ballcarrier "running for daylight" even though the planned blocking failed, the play could still succeed.

The quarterback option play uses the same theory. If the defensive end is in position to tackle the quarterback as he sweeps to the outside, the quarterback simply tosses the ball to his trailing halfback. If the defensive end crosses the line of scrimmage to defend against the lateral, the quarterback keeps the ball and turns upfield. It makes no difference how the end plays. He is always wrong.

The quarterback option play

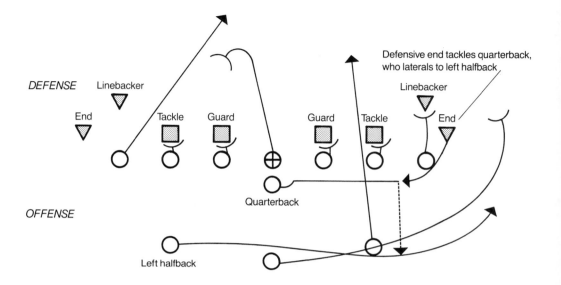

The defensive end tackles the quarterback who laterals to his halfback (A).

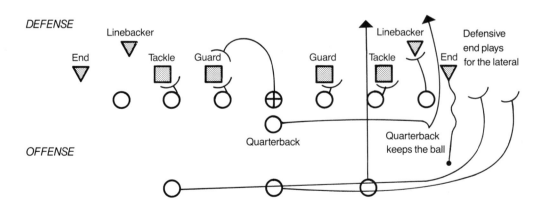

The defensive end plays for the lateral. The quarterback keeps the ball (B).

In the Single Wing, the off-tackle play, to succeed, required blocking the end out. The sweep, to succeed, required blocking the end in. The blockers' skill was basic to the success of the play.

The Single-Wing off-tackle play
The defensive end must be blocked out.

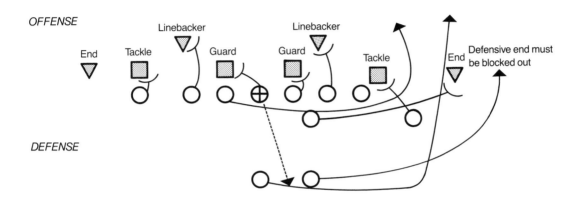

The Single-Wing sweep
The defensive end must be blocked in.

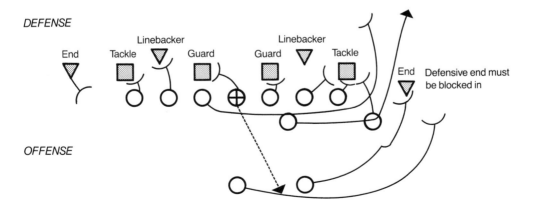

As passing skills developed, we changed our formation to the Wing-T. By using the split end, we had a receiver who could always get downfield to run a pass pattern. The wingback, too, could be an effective pass receiver as well as a blocker and a ballcarrier. The formation enabled us to throw the ball more easily, and it still maintained almost all of the elements of our basic Split-T attack.

The Wing-T formation
The wingback can block, go out as a pass receiver or run reverses. The split end spreads the secondary and is an effective pass receiver.

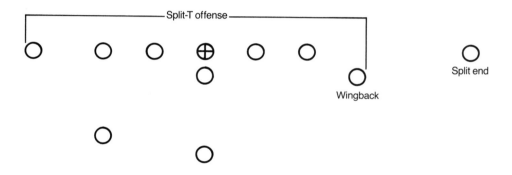

It should be emphasized that the success of our attack was always dependent on our team's ability to change the point of attack AFTER the ball was snapped. That remains the key to running any successful offense today.

In the years since I was an active coach, offensive philosophy has continued along the same lines. Modern teams use an increasing number of pass receivers detached from the formation, and the passers and receivers get more efficient every season. The fundamental element of offensive football, however, always will remain the same. The offensive blockers, particularly the linemen, must be able to get and maintain contact with their opponents without being overpowered. These men are the true "skill" players.

During my career, the most far-reaching, fundamental change in offensive football was the advent of "two-platoon" play—free substitution. In recent years, a football squad has become in fact three well-defined units—the offensive team; the defensive team; and the special teams.

This rule change has enabled more boys to participate as their special physical skills are utilized at every position. Two-platoon football has, however, diminished, to a degree, some of the fundamental factors that in one-platoon football played the dominant role in a team's failure or success.

In two-platoon football, each player uses his natural abilities to excel at his position. He is not required to do things that do not come naturally to him.

In one-platoon football, every man had to play both offense and defense. That required him to learn to do things that did not come naturally to him. For example, the offensive center, in addition to playing as a blocker, had to function as a linebacker. Offensive backs had to learn to play in the defensive secondary. The discipline required made, in my view, the learning experience much more meaningful.

One clear-cut example makes the case. I did not care, when I was a coach, to have a 4.4 sprinter-receiver get behind the secondary and catch a touchdown pass if the same man on the next play could not line up, cover the kickoff, and then play effectively as a defensive back. This required skills that today's sprinter-receiver probably does not have.

In spite of my views, I am sure that the two-platoon game is here to stay. It has its faults, I think, but it results in a more sophisticated, interesting game for the spectators as well as the players.

Much has been written about the "life-learning values" of participating in football. I am convinced that those factors are real. A boy should play the game because it can make such a contribution to his personal discipline and attitude toward every phase of life.

The first and most important lesson learned is to defeat physical fear. Any young man who starts to play the game is subconsciously and consciously afraid of the violent physical contact demanded by the sport. In its truest sense, football is a "collision sport." Violent contact cannot be avoided. Yet, through the proper teaching and coaching progression, fear can be overcome.

Teaching young football players to overcome the "fear factor" is similar to teaching a young boy to dive. The first time any young man is asked by his teacher or parents to dive into the water, he is frightened because he is facing the unknown. He does not know how to dive. By being taught first to fall forward from the side of the pool into the water without fear, the diver, through successive stages, learns to use his legs to dive into the pool head-first. Once

As President John F. Kennedy told the author, no society is stronger than the "vigor and vitality of its citizens."

this is accomplished, he can progress to the execution of fancy dives such as the swan, jackknife, and somersault.

Football players go through the same progression in learning to overcome their fear of contact. They are taught the "hitting position." They block against a dummy or passive opponent. Then they block against a three-quarter effort by the defensive man. Finally, they learn to block against an opponent who is going full-speed in an effort to avoid the block. Through that progression, the boy, by learning to execute his fundamentals, will overcome his innate fears. He will learn to enjoy the physical combat.

In my unprejudiced opinion, participation in football is the greatest overall learning experience any boy can have.

First, he must develop his own body—learn to run and build his muscles so he can execute the basic skills of the game.

Next, he must learn to play his individual position. That teaches him the dependence he has on his teammates. As noted above, no man alone can ever succeed in football.

Those attributes are needed by anyone who desires to lead a productive life.

When I served as consultant on physical fitness to President John F. Kennedy, he told me on numerous occasions that no society was stronger than the "vigor and vitality of its citizens." That is true for all of us. We do not function any better in our personal lives than our good health, vigor, and vitality allow. What we are able to do is based on our physical well-being. Every football player recognizes that his ability is determined by his physical condition. Through the experience of playing, he carries that conviction throughout his life in all of his personal pursuits.

Football players also learn to make their best effort on every play. That, too, carries over. The former football player will be dedicated and, no matter what job he may be required to do, he will make his best effort on a continuing basis.

Every institution in our society—businesses, churches, civic clubs, the armed forces, etc.—requires, for success, the continuing best effort of each member of the organization.

Football players have learned through their playing experience that they are interdependent. They know from experience that success cannot be achieved unless they function as a member of the "team." Thus, playing football does in reality "build men." It is a learning experience that should be part of every young man's education.